D0672312

PLAYBOY'S BOOK OF LIMERICKS

PLAYBOY'S BOOK OF LIMERICKS

Edited by
Clifford M. Crist

Castle Books, Inc.

COVER DESIGN BY HAL SIEGEL

PUBLISHED SIMULTANEOUSLY IN THE UNITED STATES AND CANADA BY PLAYBOY PRESS, CHICAGO, ILLINOIS. PRINTED IN THE UNITED STATES OF AMERICA. LIBRARY OF CONGRESS CATALOG CARD NUMBER: 78-187403. FIRST EDITION.

THIS EDITION PUBLISHED BY CASTLE BOOKS, INC.
BY ARRANGEMENT WITH PLAYBOY PRESS,
A DIVISION OF PLAYBOY ENTERPRISES, INC.

Dedicated To
THE SOCIETY
OF THE
FIFTH LINE

TABLE OF CONTENTS

INTRODUCTION

If you say to a literate guy, "Limericks!," comes a gleam in his eye and he quotes one or two; if he can't tell a few, then, beware; he's an enemy spy.

(Anon, famous composer of limericks)

As one literary genre after another has, in our decadent civilization, gone sterile, the limerick has retained its pristine elegance and its caustic wit, as this generous collection of limericks will demonstrate.

A host of the traditional, familiar limericks are here. These are the precious heirlooms of our talented ancestors who, often by oral tradition in the days of fuddy-duddy censorship, have bequeathed them to posterity, as did the ancient troubadours their precious poetry.

Classic limericks have an aura of timeless respectability about them. They have received the equivalent of Oscars, Tonys, or Emmys and inspire among limerick-lovers as much awe and admiration as do, among God-fearing men, breasty movie stars and muscled athletes. They should be told with due reverence to all, old and young. And the younger the audience, the better, for this truly magnificent form of modern literature is blatantly ignored in college curricula, even at the graduate level, although it is a "tit-bit" more heady than pot, more puissant than liquor, more sensuous than secret vice, and only slightly inferior to the act of love itself.

Scattered throughout the book are several hundred new limericks never before published between hard covers. Some of these have been composed by old hands, some by talented newcomers. So fascinating is the art of making limericks, once it has been ventured, that today's beginner speedily becomes tomorrow's expert. Let the fiendish practice get its grip, and then try and stop at composing just one limerick.

It is the aspiration of every limerick-lover to compose, during a lifetime of indolence and folly, at least one perfect limerick that will survive him and become a classic, a part of the immortal canon. Several of the new limericks in this collection bid fair to receive such an accolade, to the glory of the composers who, like so many authors of yore, must remain anonymous. All hail to their success!

A first-rate limerick needs the humorous touch of Robert Benchley, the mordant wit of Oscar Wilde, the shock value of an X-rated film. So potent is the limerick's secret power that many hostesses forbid it, for once the guests start telling limericks, it is goodbye to gossip, ecology, politics, and furtive dalliance in the kitchen or the greenhouse.

The basic requirement for great limericks is that they be humorous. What is Humor? one may rightly ask. Many serious attempts have been made to explain it and to define it by categories or cases. One intriguing theory claims that all humor can be boiled down to three situations: (1) witnessing another being cuckolded, or criticized in the midst of his lovemaking; (2) witnessing another being robbed or (the biter bit) caught up in his own machinations; (3) witnessing another taking a pratfall or suffering an equally deflating experience. In each of these cases lies the basic weapon of humor: the witness laughing at what happens to *another*. Freud demonstrated how pleasant it is to witness happening to other people anything we would not wish to happen to us.

One of the greatest delights of the early two-reel comedies was to see a pompous person (and if he wore a high hat, so much the better) strutting down the street, then get a quick shot of a youth eating a banana and pointedly throwing the peel behind him upon the sidewalk. As the camera pans back to the pompous strutter, the audience begins to chortle, stomp feet, and whistle in anticipation. And the audience is never disappointed; the pompous man *does* step on the banana peel, he *does* take a horrendous header, and the audience roars its delight.

Such, perhaps at a slightly more modest decibel level, is the reception of great limericks, with their impeccable Fifth Lines, the banana peels of life. The first four lines serve but to prepare the audience, the Fifth Line delivers the whammy. For an amorous swain, confident and cocky at his work, to be interrupted in his ardor by the lady's remark in the Fifth Line, "You've got it all in but the head" or "This won't be much of a sin" or "You mean it ain't your finger?" reveals there is always a banana peel lurking for the unwary.

The origin of the word *limerick* is unknown, although there have been many suggestions. It is generally acknowledged that it does not have anything to do with County Limerick in Ireland or the town of Limerick or with the earl of Limerick and his charming duchess (who is just a dear friend). Traces of the form have been found in early literature, in folk ballads, in Shakespeare. Whatever these origins may have been and what influence they have had on the modern limerick's form,[1] it is commonly accepted that these little verses began to be called

[1] For a historical and scholarly description of the origins and growth of the limerick, as well as a very solid bibliography, see William S. Baring-Gould's brilliant introduction to his *The Lure of the Limerick* (New York: Clarkson N. Potter, 1967).

limericks around the middle of the nineteenth century.

In 1846, Edward Lear, the father of the limerick, published his *A Book of Nonsense*. In all, Lear composed over two hundred limericks. For him, the limerick was in the tradition of his light verse, a gossamer and airy (and clean) bit of whimsy, faultlessly versified. Lear often coined his own words, and the puckish quality of "The Owl and the Pussycat" is everywhere in evidence. However, in almost all of Lear's limericks, the rhyme (last) word of the first line is repeated as the last word of the Fifth Line. But many have overlooked the fact that Lear on occasion did use three *different* rhyme words, as in the following:

There was a Young Lady whose eyes
Were unique as to color and size;
When she opened them wide,
People all turned aside,
And started away in surprise.

Admittedly, Lear's last line is not very humorous. But the use of three different rhyme words contains the germ of what was to come. It remained, near the turn of the century, for the Fifth Line to evolve into the coruscating gem it is today. At about the same time the limerick turned obscene. My God! How its popularity grew!

Early dissemination of the limerick, in no small measure due to the increasing obscenity, was largely oral, as it so often still is today. Consequently, many of the older limericks have numerous variants. The man who "put it in double" may come from Ghent or from Kent. Variants are especially common in the Fifth Line. The young man from Racine, who invented that remarkable machine for which, it seems, he never got a patent, has a number of Fifth Lines, to wit:

> Entertaining itself in between.
> And guaranteed used by the queen.
> With a drip-pot to catch all the cream.
> And jerked itself off in between.
> The God-damndest thing ever seen.
> With attachments for those in between.

Who is to say which of these is the best? Why spoil the delight of the experts who, after the limerick has been told in one version, then proceed to recite, at carefully timed intervals, alternate Fifth Lines, to the increasing hilarity of the audience?

There have been many attempts, and not always commendable ones, to improve upon the classics. This is another cause for variant versions. The Racine limerick is among the most widely known and recited ones, so it is not surprising that it has such a wealth of Fifth Lines. One should not be too hard on those who tinker with the classics. Have you never felt the urge to add some obscenity to *American Gothic?*

Variants also may arise because the reciter forgets the exact rhyme word and coins an equivalent (Kent for Ghent). It is even easier to forget the exact words of lines three and four and an impromptu version is created, sometimes superior to the original. But one man's favorite may not be another's. Do not interrupt the laughter at the end of a limerick with a pedantic, "No, no! It goes. . . ." It is far better, as the laughter dies down, to add your version as an afterthought. You may get a bigger laugh and even reap the pleasure of seeing the original teller of the limerick furtively jot down your line.

The purpose of the limerick, as already mentioned, is to amuse and entertain. Some of the classics have been deliberately excluded from this collection, mainly because they are witless and in poor taste, despite their considerable popularity. They more often receive a supercilious snicker than a hearty guffaw. The banana peel has lost some of its slickness. Such limericks may help explain why little old ladies do not enjoy limericks and, at the first one, take off for the loo, presumably to relace their tennis shoes.

In the attempt to find challenging and novel rhyme words, astute limerick researchers have used most of the countries and cities of the world. It would require a geographical expert to locate every such place correctly on the map. Newcomers to the field are sometimes surprised to discover that the most popular limerick country is Peru. What is the fatal attraction of this innocent little country? The answer lies in the number of common words that rhyme with it: *canoe, do, coo, woo, Jew, pew, new, threw, blew, spew, stew, gnu, flu, through, sou, blue, two, few, to, cockatoo, zoo, true, glue;* all these have been used, and *screw you too!* For similar reasons, limericks about Bombay, France, Khartoum, Madras, Madrid, and Siam abound.

If the limerick has nearly exhausted the countries and cities of the world, what about the *dramatis personae* of the limerick? As might be expected, there is almost no profession that has not been honored, almost no job, be it ever so humble, that has not been touched upon. The army, navy, air force and marines; the medical profession (doctors, dentists, surgeons, morticians, obstetricians, even Dr. Freud); musicians ranging from the aloof maestro to a simple flutist, plus a goodly company of famous composers; artists, painters, writers; world-famous figures from Gandhi and Napoleon to De Gaulle and Governor Wallace. From less exalted ranks come athletes, cowboy and gaucho, baker and barber, plumber, tailor, jeweler, gardener, teacher and student, seamstress, militant females, a cabby's wife, even a Hindu mahout. The one profession seldom glorified in the limerick is the legal one. But then, the law is so seldom humorous.

Far and away the most popular subject for limericks is the clergy. There are over three hundred in existence that deal with the men and women of the Church, many of them included in this volume. Very few are complimentary. According to the majority of limericks, the practitioners of religion practice nefarious practices! But evil is in the eye of the beholder.

The majority of clerical limericks are concerned with the lowly: the curate, the monk, the parson, the preacher, and the vicar appear more than a dozen times and the misunderstood priest more than twenty-five. The total picture they create is a pretty shabby and scandalous one. Only on rare occasions does a limerick treat the man of God gently or even with grudging respect. Most of the participants are meek about their sins and accept their condemnation humbly, but this monotony is relieved by an occasional rakish and defiant servant of the Church.

The curate is criticized, mostly by women, for his lack of ardor. The monk is often pictured as licentious, as are the nuns. The parson is an object of scorn; the preacher suffers from constipation and flatulation and preaches at such length his faithful flock threatens to stuff him with firecrackers. The vicar gets more sympathetic treatment, although he is warned of strangulation if he insists upon singing at services.

The poor priest is the common butt for all dissatisfaction with religious practices. He is the link between the people and the Church. Again and again he is pictured as committing various acts of depravity, being immoral in the confessional, afflicted with venereal disease and, with all that, stingy and critical to excess.

So much for the lower ranks. Limericks mention all those high in the clerical Establishment but they are treated with due respect; the pope, the cardinal, the archbishop, although this worthy, as we descend the ladder, is criticized for acts of fornication.

The main culprit is the bishop. We are now far enough down the hierarchical line to find the scapegoat for the Establishment, as the priest was for the lesser clergy. There exist some three dozen limericks devoted to bishops and in them he continually gets his comeuppance. He commits frequent intercourse (and, unlike others, is very adept at it, managing thirteen with the wife of the dean), practices incest and miscegenation, even keeps young owls for immoral purposes. As a price for his sins, he suffers from elephantiasis.

So much for the clergy. Where there is smoke there is often a friar. But it must be pointed out that most of the accusations against the clergy could probably have been made against Napoleon, Henry James, or Toulouse-Lautrec. And about many other people we know!

The limerick is the whole universe in microcosm. Future sociologists and psychologists will study it as a fascinating aspect of social psychology. It is a *Who's Who* of social, artistic, and political fame. It immortalizes scandalous gossip. The name of Magda Lupescu is on more tongues than that of the king she was under and the limerick about Elizabeth Barrett might just possibly be better known than most of her poetry. Rose Madder is as well known as Titian, and that famous statue of Phidias is familiar to thousands who have never seen it. And Gloria has made the band at the Waldorf Astoria forever immortal.

Many people aspire to compose limericks of their own, despite the notion that such persons are admittedly crazy and charlatans to boot. It is not easy to compose a limerick, but even great poets had their difficulties. Those who do not possess a well-developed sense of rhythm and meter should devote their energies to declaiming limericks, spewing them forth like veritable geysers of wit for an enchanted throng. But if one has the rhyming ability and a modicum of waggery, best wishes!

There are some general bits of advice that may be helpful to the beginner. In the first place, try starting with the Fifth Line. This line is the crux of the good limerick. If you do not have a great one at the start, you are likely to waste your talents on four good lines, only to find that the limerick goes down the drain for lack of the Fifth Line, like a drama with two good acts and a wretched third one. The Fifth Line may be almost anything: the punch line of a story, or an outrageous pun, or a switch on some current slogan or famous name, or just some little line of your own that scans perfectly and scintillates with wit. As a test of creative ability and genius, several limericks are included in this collection with Fifth Lines missing.

The first and second lines usually work in tandem to set the scene, geographically and physically. They should build up an aura of suspense, impending excitement, or doom (throw down the banana peel). It is sometimes necessary to invent a proper name or a place to provide a sufficient number of rhyme words. If someone challenges your geography, just say it is a town in Uttar Pradesh or a village due north of Ulan Bator. The classic structure of "There was a young lady (fellow) from . . ." has given way to various opening lines, such as "Said a civil rights worker named Dot," or "A worried young man from Stamboul."

The third and fourth lines may be needed to further the plot, whetting the appetite for the denouement. These two lines often determine the final elegance of the limerick. They should be a pyrotechnical display of the composer's power of language and poetical instinct. How charming to find lines like "While in her interstices / Lurked a far worse disease" and "The weather's too sultry / To commit adult'ry." *Summa cum laude!*

Limericks must be worked over and over. Often they must be put aside to await a more benevolent gesture from the Muse, even thrown away entirely and a new start made. Nothing does more harm to a limerick than a line that limps. It can never be excused. But if the main idea for the limerick is sparkling, witty, and novel and the rhymes good, it will eventually work out and the thrill of the completed gem is one of the Nine Joys of the World. As a toiler in the vineyard once wrote:

You labor from midnight to morn,
Consuming a gallon of corn.
The last line comes neatly,
You pass out completely,
And thus is a limerick born.

Endless variations of the standard five-line limerick have been perpetrated: two-liners, three-liners, six-liners; limericks with extra long Fifth Lines and extra short ones; with rhymes such as St. Bees, wasp and hornet; with surprise endings; with endless repetition, such as the young lady from Spain (or from Maine) who did it again and again and again and again. . . . There is a limerick composed entirely of the syllable "da" scanning perfectly for four lines and all of the Fifth Line except the last syllable, which is any four-letter word desired. There is a limerick beginning "There was a young man from Racine / Birmingham, Wheeling, Moline," continuing to the end with places made famous by limericks. There are also a few limericks in Latin, French, German, Spanish, and one in Russian and another in Swahili. All of them prove conclusively that English is the mother tongue of the limerick.

These little tricks aside, there has been little change in the limerick form for over a hundred years. This may very well be for the best, considering what innovation has done to the modern novel, drama, and poetry. One variation has appeared. It consists of a number of third and fourth lines within the classical body of the limerick. There may be two sets or several. It permits detailed background, intense character development and delineation, a complicated story, while at the same time it taxes the composer's poetic talents. Since these added sequences are all in the middle of the limerick, they are referred to as The Inner Limerick. The following is one of the longest, and even if it does not become popular it may triple traveling by air:

A voluptuous maiden named Wright
Took a 747 one night.
The salesman beside her
Was first to bestride her.
He found her too ample,
But left a small sample,
Though he nearly was trapped
When his seat belt unsnapped.

Up front, a musician
Used finger coition,
And while she was coming
From Wagner kept humming;
Then put in his wienie
To strains of Rossini,
And came to his glory
With *Il Trovatore*.

A young priest on her right
Sodomized her all night.
He came like a rabbit
And deplored his habit.

A judge seated in back
Took a leisurely whack,
And when done, said drolly,
"This'll hurt your parole."

A Frenchman 'cross the aisle
Watched it all with a smile,
And when each one was done,
Said in French, "Vive le fun!"

A young lad from First Class
Stole a pinch of her ass.
He'll remember for weeks
Those soft velvety cheeks,
And forever, perchance,
How he came in his pants.

The stewardess rushed through,
"Coffee, tea, milk . . . or screw!"
But when she looked over
Those white breasts of Dover,
She gave out a loud scream
And containers of cream.

When the Captain came by
There was nought left to try.
He grumbled, "No joking,
There's been too much poking;
I'll turn off NO SMOKING,
And light up NO FOKING."

Now Wright knows what it means, Maiden Flight.

Will this meet the rigid standards of limericists? Or is it too frilly? It might be good fun if sung with piano or guitar accompaniment, the first set of Inner Lines sung as a solo, the second set as a duet, the third as a trio, the fourth as a quartette. And so on, or repeat for the last four sets. Everyone joins in for the Fifth Line. The accompanist should add a soupçon of Wagner, Rossini, and the "Anvil Chorus" at the appropriate moment and feel free to embellish any of the sets as his genius sees fit. It is a challenge.

There are a couple of novelties in this book. Following the limericks, which are arranged alphabetically by rhyme word as a dictionary, are several pages printed with (five) blank lines in limerick form. These are for favorite limericks omitted from the collection as well as for limericks of your own creation. As the pages are filled you become the owner of the only book of its kind in existence. There are also several pages containing limericks with the Fifth Line to be supplied by you, and with additional spaces for other Fifth Lines, where talented guests may write their versions, thus preserving their inventions for posterity and creating a novel Guest Book.

There is a selective Bibliography of limerick collections and a Roll of Honor of additional famous composers and newcomers included in this volume. To facilitate locating limericks, there is an Index of the rhyme word of the Fifth Line (with the rhyme word of the first line in parentheses) for those who remember the Fifth Line only.

Thanks and appreciation go first of all to the master of modern limerick research, Gershon Legman, whose *The Limerick* (see Bibliography) is not only the largest but also the most carefully researched and annotated compilation; it has over a hundred pages of notes and variants. It is the canon for all limericists. For all authors and editors of limericks, humble gratitude not only for their great personal contributions but also for the inspiration they have given over the years and the standards of excellence they have set. Since so many limericks are spread orally, it is not always possible to give credit and acknowledgment for every limerick. The editor and publisher offer sincere apologies to any authors whose limericks may have unintentionally been included in this volume without written or oral permission.

Finally, heartfelt thanks to the authors of the many original limericks in this collection. May these be recited wherever limerick-lovers meet. May new generations continue to carry high the great tradition of "accordion pleats full of airy conceits."

New York City / Summer, 1971 *C. M. C.*

LIMERICKS

abstention

A matron who favored abstention
Had breasts of unequal dimension.
When woo'd by her hubby,
She withheld the large bubby,
Thus causing domestic dissension.

Ada

A young taxidermist from Ada,
Whose wife said he'd often betrayed her,
Was sued for divorce
For mounting a horse,
A moose and a goose and a 'gator.

Adair

There was a young man named Adair,
Who was having his girl on the stair.
When the banister broke,
He doubled his stroke,
And polished her off in mid-air.

Adam

In the Garden of Eden lay Adam,
Caressing the mons of his madam;
And he thought with elation,
That in all of creation,
There were only two balls, and he had 'em.

adroit

Though at lying my aunt is adroit,
I don't see what she hopes to exploit.
She claims she was zood
In Kalamascrood,
But I know it took place in Detroit.

Aenos

There was a young woman from Aenos
Who came to our party as Venus.
We told her how rude
'Twas to come there quite nude,
And we brought her a leaf from the green-h'us.

Alaska

There was a young girl from Alaska,
Who could, and she would, if you asked her.
But she thought she was nice,
And so high was her price,
That no one could have her, save Jesus H. Christ.
(And, occasionally, John Jacob Astor.)

Algiers

There was an old bey of Algiers,
Who said to his harem, "My dears!
You may think it odd o' me,
But I've given up sodomy;
Tonight there'll be fucking!" (Loud cheers.)

Alice

A gifted young showgirl named Alice
Could pick up loose coins with her phallus,
But it couldn't make change,
Which narrowed her range
And kept her from playing the Palace.

Alice

Nymphomaniacal Alice
Used a dynamite stick for a phallus.
They found her vagina
In North Carolina
And her ass-hole in Buckingham Palace.

Alsace

There was a young man from Alsace,
Whose balls were constructed of brass.
When he clanged them together,
They played "Stormy Weather"
And lightning came out of his ass.
(And on Sundays, Bach's B Minor Mass.)

Although

Said a greedy old piggie, "Although
The sows leave when they've eaten enough,
I still squat in the slough,
With my snout in the trough;
I will never admit I am through."

anchor

A sailor at Bangor cast anchor,
With syphilis, buboes and chancre.
All this, and some more,
He'd got from one whore,
So he wrote her a letter to thank her.

Andante Cantabile

While humming "Andante Cantabile,"
A sculptor constructed a mobile.
When it failed to revolve,
He made this resolve:
"I really must build them more wobile."

Anheuser

There was a young girl named Anheuser,
Who boasted no man could surprise her.
Pabst took a chance,
Found Schlitz in her pants,
And now she is sadder Budweiser.

Arabia

There was a young girl from Arabia,
Who committed immodest behavia.
She sat in each class,
With her skirt round her ass,
And smooched at the prof with her labia.

Aries

A young lady born under Aries
Consults the stars each time she marries.
Although she gets hope
From each horoscope,
Her husbands turn out to be fairies.

arrack

Sakumbe, when full of arrack,
Slapped Cohen, his friend, on the back,
And cried, "You're all right!
Though your skin may be white,
At heart you are thoroughly black."

Asgalun

The monarch of old Asgalun
Was said to be struck by the moon.
He leaped from his bed,
With his rump painted red,
And cried, "I'm a Kushite baboon!"

askew

An old linotype went askew,
With its naked machinery in view.
In this state of undress,
It made love to the press,
Saying gently, "Etaoin shrdlu."

Astor

There was a young woman named Astor,
Whose clothes fit her tight as a plaster.
When she happened to sneeze,
She felt a cold breeze,
And knew she had met with disaster.

Astor

While befuddled with booze, Mr. Astor
Made a pass at a statue of plaster.
When informed of his error,
His mind filled with terror.
"What a blessing," he said, "I'm not faster."

A-Tasket

When you think of "A-Tisket, A-Tasket,"
Remember the woman named Baskett,
Who contrived a good stunt
To put up a front
And carried her teats in a basket.

Australia

There was a young man from Australia,
Who painted his bung like a dahlia.
The drawing was fine,
The color divine . . .
But the scent—Ah! that was a failure.

Avery

There was an old fellow named Avery
Whose habits were highly unsavory.
With devilish howls
He deflowered young owls,
Which he kept in an underground aviary.

Babbit

Two biologists, Hansen and Babbit,
Crossed a camel one time with a rabbit.
The offspring was jumpy,
And frightfully humpy,
And had a lascivious habit.

bad

A young man from Ward said, "Too bad,
There's nothing in sight but a lad.
I'll just have to retrench
On this yen for a wench,
But it does make me feel like a cad."

Bäger

A German musician named Bäger,
Spurred on by a very high wager,
Proceeded to fart
The complete oboe part
Of a Haydn octet in A-major.

ball

It's my own fault I just have one ball,
And it's lucky I have one at all.
In the place I was sittin'
I shouldn't have written
My phone number up on that wall.

Bangor

There was a young lady from Bangor,
Who slept while the ship lay at anchor.
She awoke with dismay
To hear the mate say,
"Let's lift up the top-sheet and spanker."

Barnard

The eminent Christiaan Barnard
Has labeled "A baseless canard"
That, by transplanting epoxy
Into older men's jocks, he
Can cause them once more to get hard.

Baroda

There was a young girl of Baroda,
Who built a new kind of pagoda.
The walls of its halls
Were hung with the balls
And the tools of the fools who bestrode her.

Barr

A girl undertaker named Barr
Carried her independence too far.
When business was laggin',
She took her long wagon
And started up *Hearse* rent-a-car.

Bates

There was a young lady named Bates,
Who was cursed from birth by the Fates.
She wished that she could,
And feared that she would,
And that was the end of her dates.

Batonger

There was a young girl from Batonger,
Who was jazzing herself with a conger.
When asked how it feels
To be pleasured by eels,
She replied, "Like a man, only longer."

Bay Head

There was a young man from Bay Head,
Who took a young lady to bed.
He hoped she would kiss,
Climax him to bliss;
She read an old PLAYBOY instead.

Beal

A modest young lady named Beal
Once protected herself with great zeal,
But when she'd been wedded,
The thing that she'd dreaded
Was a boon of enormous appeal.

Beers

Said a white-haired old lady named Beers,
As she balled with a quintet of queers,
"As God is my witness,
This is the shit'nest
Gang-bang I've had in nine years."

begat

There was a young girl who begat
Three babies named Nat, Tat, and Pat.
It was fun in the breeding,
But hell in the feeding;
She found there was no tit for Tat.

beginning

God's plan had a hopeful beginning,
But man spoiled his chances by sinning.
We trust that the story
Will end in God's glory,
But, at present, the other side's winning.

Belgravia

There was a young man from Belgravia,
Who cared neither for God nor his Saviour.
He walked down the Strand
With his prick in his hand,
And was had up for indecent behaviour.

Ben

A bibliophile, name of Ben,
Had lustful designs on a hen,
Who, with pleasure and pride,
Most obligingly cried,
With a flip of her feathers, "Say when!"

Benares

A nudist resort at Benares
Took a midget in, all unawares,
But he made members weep
For he just couldn't keep
His nose out of private affairs.

Bengal

There was a young man of Bengal,
Who swore he had only one ball.
Then two little bitches,
They pulled down his britches,
And found that he had none at all.

Bengal

There was a young man of Bengal
Who went to a fancy-dress ball.
Just for a whim,
He dressed up as a quim,
And was had by the dog in the hall.

Berlin

There was a young girl in Berlin
Who was raped by an elderly Finn.
Though he diddled his best
And screwed her with zest,
She kept asking, "Hey, Pop! Is it in?"

Big Dell

There was a young athlete, Big Dell,
Whose tool was too large for his belle.
While the surgeon was clipping,
The knife started slipping—
Now he's called by his friends Little Nell.

Bill

A mechanical marvel named Bill
Had a tool which was shaped like a quill.
With this scholarly dink
He could squirt purple ink
And write, draw, or color at will.

Birmingham

There were two young ladies from
Birmingham,
And this is the story concerning 'em.
They lifted the frock,
And played with the cock,
Of the bishop while he was confirming 'em.

But the bishop was nobody's fool;
He'd been sent to a large public school.
So he took down his britches
And skizzled the bitches
With his eight-inch Episcopal tool.

It is true that the bishop of Birmingham
Diddled these girls while confirming 'em.
'Mid liturgical chants,
He took down his pants
And released the Episcopal sperm in 'em.

Now the clergy of Birmingham just heard
That their broad-minded bishop got plastered.
The occasion was this:
He was told by a miss
He'd begot an Episcopal bastard.

But this bishop did nothing amiss
In conducting these lasses to bliss.
May the Church ne'er unfrock
His Episcopal cock,
But keep it, a relic to kiss.

Blanche

There was a young lady named Blanche,
Who screwed all the boys at the ranch.
After sexing all day
'Til their pricks wore away,
She demanded nocturnal revanche.

Blum

A most passionate spinster named Blum
Found a lad who was eager but dumb.
With her hand on his knee,
She begged him, "Come and see!"
He replied, "Don't you mean see and come?"

boast

I confess that I'm not one to boast
Of orgiastic delights . . . but a toast
To the stupendous ability
Of my once proud facility,
I think I remember . . . almost.

boist

A Brooklyn boy ready to boist,
Shacked up wit' a French goil, his foist.
When she said, "Ah! Mon cher!"
He replied, "Stop right dere!
Would you radder we fuckt or convoist?"

boisterous

There was a young abbess, too boisterous,
Who was sent off posthaste from the cloisters.
She poured vichyssoise
On the salade niçoise,
And Bavarian cream on the oysters.

Bombay

There was a young girl from Bombay
Who was put in a family way,
By the mate of a lugger,
An ignorant bugger,
Who always spelled cunt with a *k*.

Bombay

There was a young man from Bombay,
Who was jazzing his girl in a sleigh,
But the cold was so frigid
It froze his balls rigid,
And all he could shoot was frappé.

Bombay

There was a young man of Bombay,
Who modeled a cunt out of clay,
But the heat of his prick
Turned the clay into brick,
Which wore all his foreskin away.

Bone

There was a young dentist named Bone,
Who catered to ladies alone.
In a mood of depravity,
He filled the wrong cavity.
My God! How his business has grown!

bonhomie

When Pan, full of classical bonhomie,
Met a maiden, she cried, "Don't get onna me!
And the goats I keep, too,
I forbid you to screw;
I have just read a book . . . Deuteronomy!"

boot

'Twas the thirteenth, and Friday to boot,
When he first wore his new Pucci suit,
And before the next morn
It was spotted and torn,
But his girl thought his root was still cute.

Bordeaux

A clumsy young clod from Bordeaux
Was jazzing a girl in St. Lô.
They fell from her rack,
He stepped on her crack,
Now he's nursing clap of the toe.

Boston

There was a young fellow from Boston,
Who drove around in an Austin.
He had room for his ass,
And a gallon of gas,
But his balls hung out and he lost 'em.

Boston

There was a young lady from Boston,
Who thought she was raped in an Austin,
But the truth is, my dears,
She sat on the gears,
And a traffic cop kicked the exhaust in.

Bough

A young writer of Verses named Bough
Ate the Loaf, drained the Jug, then yelled,
"Thou
Mak'st my life a total mess,
Singing in the Wilderness,
Hush, love, thou'st spoiled Paradise enow."

Boulder

A boastful blonde virgin from Boulder
Swore no man on earth had yet rolled her.
She was therefore dismayed
When her charms were displayed
On the front of the summer school folder.

Bract

A young trapeze-swinger named Bract
Is faced by a very grim fact:
Consider his pain
When, again and again,
He catches his wife in the act.

Bray

An indolent vicar of Bray
Spent before he withdrew, one fine day.
His wife, more alert,
Got a vaginal squirt,
And said to her spouse, "Let us spray!"

Brent

There was a young lady named Brent
Who upon a divorce was hell-bent.
"Life had been fine,"
She said, "Sex divine!"
'Til her husband got indifferent.

Brice

A leprous old bastard named Brice
Had balls that were spotted like dice.
They were worthless as could be
In the way that balls should be,
But a wonderful gambling device.

Bridget

There was a young coed named Bridget,
Whose clothes were too short for a midget.
Every lad in the class
Got a peek at her ass,
And she'd wink at the prof with her twidget.

Brighton

There was a young fellow from Brighton,
Who thought he'd at last found a tight one.
He said, "Oh, my love,
It fits like a glove!"
She replied, "You're not in the right one."

Bruges

There once was a duchess of Bruges,
Whose cunt was exceedingly huge.
Said the king, as he came,
To this spirited dame,
"Mon Dieu! Après moi, le déluge."

Bruno

There once was a gaucho named Bruno,
Who said, "Screwing is all that I do know.
A woman is fine,
A sheep is divine,
But a llama! There's numero uno!"

Bryde

There was a fat lady of Bryde
Whose shoelaces once came untied,
But she didn't dare stoop,
For fear she would poop,
And she cried and she cried and she cried.

Bryerder

There was a young trucker named Bryerder,
Who met a good harlot and hired her
To fuck between trucks,
But to truck between fucks
Made him tireder and tireder and tireder.

Bulgaria

There was a young man of Bulgaria
Who took down his pants in an area.
Said Mary to cook,
"Oh! Do come and look.
Did you ever see anything hairier?"

bursar

There once was an indigent bursar
Whose wife was a swearer and curser,
So when she would start
To fume and to fart,
He would let the fart bitch . . . and vice versa!

Burunda

A barbarous critic from Burunda
Committed a grave social bulunda,
By having emissions
Before several Titians
In the Andrew J. Mellon rotunda.

Buster

An effete young sailor named Buster
Had pricks in a multiple cluster.
He could have an erection
In any direction,
And afterwards serve as a duster.

Bynum

A newly-wed husband named Bynum
Asked his bride to please sixty-nine him.
When she shook her head,
He sighed and then said,
"Well, if we can't lick 'em, let's join 'em."

Byzance

Theodora, the queen of Byzance,
Is remembered for having hot pants.
At one soirée de luxe
She took on three dukes,
Two eunuchs, one ape, and four aunts.

Calcutta

There was an old man of Calcutta,
Who had an unfortunate stutter.
"I would like," he once said,
"Some bub-bub-bub-bread
And some bub-bub-bub-bub-bub-bub-butter."

Cancer

A zoophile born under Cancer,
Joined up as a cavalry lancer,
But he died of despair
When his favorite mare
Was replaced by a motorized panzer.

Cape

A lusty old man from the Cape
Kept his mattress in excellent shape
With pubic hairs plucked
From women he'd fucked
In the course of a lifetime of rape.

Cape

There was an old man of the Cape
Who buggered a Barbary ape.
Said the ape, "Sir, your prick
Is too long and too thick,
And something is wrong with the shape."

Cape Hatteras

There was a young man from Cape Hatteras,
Who kept poking holes through the matteras.
He said, with a wail,
"It's me wife's narrow tail,
I'll have to get one with a fatter ass."

Cape Horn

There was a young man from Cape Horn,
Who wished he had never been born.
And he wouldn't have been,
If his father had seen
That the end of the rubber was torn.

Capri

There was a fat wench of Capri
Who tumbled one day in the sea.
She returned from the splash
With a shark in her gash,
And her face was transfigured with glee.

carouse

Two lovers went out to carouse,
Without waiting the marital vows.
Their bliss was so sweet
They had sex in the street—
Which caused a slight raising of brows.

Carr

There once was a kiddie named Carr
Who found a man laying his mar.
Said he, with a snicker,
As he watched the guy stick her,
"You do it much faster than par."

Cawnpore

There was a young man of Cawnpore
Whose tool was so awfully sore
From slapping and rubbing,
And pulling and drubbing,
It was useless for what it was for.

Chase

Said an elegant widow named Chase,
As she peed in a squat Thracian vase,
"The heat of the museum
Titillates my perineum—
And it looks like my late husband's face."

chest

My knockers are up on my chest,
Which good Mother Nature has blessed.
My boy friends can steal
A slow or quick feel,
Which I think is all for the best.

Chester

A young maiden got married in Chester;
Her mother, she kissed her and blessed her,
And said, "You're in luck;
He's a marvelous fuck.
I know, for I've had him in Leicester."

Chester

There was a young lady of Chester
Who fell in love with a jester.
Her breath came out hotly
At sight of his motley,
But the head on his wand most impressed her.

Chichester

There was a young lady from Chichester
Whose beauty made saints in their niches stir.
As she knelt at her Mass,
The lines of her ass
Made the bishop of Chichester's britches stir.

China

There was a young preacher from China
Who loved boys but thought birds diviner.
But he gets no tail;
In fact, he's in jail,
Being charged with corrupting a mynah.

Citeaux

A horny young monk of Citeaux
Used to cool his hot rod in the snow,
But no matter how frigid,
The thing remained rigid,
Popping off when it got two below.

Clair

There was a young lady named Clair,
Who possessed a magnificent pair.
Or that's what I thought
'Til I saw one get caught
On a thorn and begin losing air.

Claire

When Tom had a lady named Claire,
He was the first one to get there.
She said, "Copulation
Can result in gestation,
But I swear, now you're there, I don't care."

Clarence

A remarkable fellow named Clarence
Learned self-control from his parents.
With his wife in bed nude,
He'd sit there and brood,
And practice the art of forbearance.

Clark

A lecherous fellow named Clark
Raped a bird-loving girl in the park.
A splendid surprise!
Such vigor! Such size!
And she really just came for a lark.

class

Some women of breeding and class
Who venture to picket en masse
Will quote from McLuhan
To each guy they're screwin',
And preach on the crassness of grass.

class

The new women's styles are first-class
For revealing the shapely young lass.
But tho better to view her,
It's much tougher to screw her,
With her stockings up over her ass.

Cletus

A lusty young coed named Cletus
Was excessively fond of coitus,
'Til a halfback from State
Made her period late.
Now she suffers from athlete's fetus.

cloister

As dull as the life of the cloister
(Except it's a little bit moister),
Mutatis mutandum
Non est disputandum,
There's no thrill in sex for the oyster.

Clyde

There was a young lady from Clyde,
Who was forced to become a quick bride,
For when her Pa tried her,
He found an outsider
Had not been completely outside.

Cohn

A randy young sideman named Cohn
Tied his donicker to his trombone.
Though improving his skills
On glissandos and trills,
It utterly ruined his tone.

colonel

A militant WAC, an old colonel,
Protests in a manner infernal.
Each week, without fail,
She sends a dead whale
To the Editor: *Ladies Home Journal.*

colonel

An old martinet of a colonel
Had a temper positively infernal,
And the reason for this
Was it hurt him to piss,
And his wife's services were diurnal.

congeal ya

Poor Hamlet! It's fit to congeal ya,
To see what a hard fate can deal ya.
For what did him in
Was a prick in the skin,
When the prick should have been in Ophelia.

Connaught

There was an old man of Connaught,
Whose prick was remarkably short.
When he got into bed,
An old woman said,
"This isn't a prick; it's a wart."

conversion

On the hundredth Baptist conversion,
A preacher kept urgin' a virgin.
'Til she finally gave in
When he said, "It's no sin,
As long as it's total immersion."

Cooper

Said the doc to J. Fenimore Cooper,
"Son, there's something gone wrong with your
pooper.
The Indians, I fear,
Have attacked from the rear,
While you lay in inebriate stupor."

Cora

A bellicose female named Cora
Thinks wedlock a male-devised horror,
And sub rosa screwing
Ain't what Libs are doing—
Tune in for her answer tomorrow!

Corelli

There was a fat girl named Corelli
Whose teats hung down to her belly.
She enjoyed copulation
With such animation
That she mashed all her partners to jelly.

Cork

There was a young lady from Cork
Who expected a call from the stork,
But with infinite caution
She performed an abortion
With two silver spoons and a fork.

course

When the race for the moon runs its course,
And women are sent there by force,
Will the men they embrace
In the world's outer space
Start to call making love "outercourse"?

coward

Sir Lancelot, never a coward,
Every maiden in Camelot scoured.
He even went farther
With Gwennie than Arthur;
That's when knighthood was truly deflowered.

Cox

Said an anxious young lady named Cox,
"On birth-control pills, wish a pox!
For some they may work,
But not for this jerk;
They always fall out of my box."

Crandall

An eclectic collector called Crandall
Acquired, with the aid of a vandal,
The bottled remains
Of John Maynard Keynes,
And the organs of George Frederick Handel.

Crater

A crafty cartographer, Crater,
Is rumored to be quite a satyr.
His testes alone—
To such size are they grown—
Must be viewed in projection Mercator.

crawl

Since early spring I've crept at snailish crawl
To finish this stone fence good neighbors call
Good. Now the winds the stately birches bend
And I have miles to go before I end . . .
Someone there is who doesn't love a wall.

Crete

A young ballerina from Crete
Offered stagehands all they could eat.
When one asked for a ride,
She reluctantly sighed,
"That would ruin my Nutcracker, Suite."

Crewe

A bashful young maiden of Crewe
Found an elephant's wang in her stew.
Said the waiter, "Don't shout,
And wave it about,
Or the rest will be wanting one, too."

cried

There was a young outlaw who cried
When he hadn't a boy by his side.
And as for his moll,
She slept with a doll—
That's the Ballad of Bonnie and Clyde.

Croft

There was a young vicar named Croft
Who played with his organ (and oft),
But afraid of a lapse,
If he played in the apse;
Or the bishop might rave,
If he played in the nave;
Or that he might falter,
If too near the altar;
And afraid he'd be whipped,
If he slipped in the crypt;
He transplanted it up to the loft.

Croft

There was a young woman of Croft,
Who played with herself in a loft,
Having reasoned that candles
Could never cause scandals,
Besides which, they did not go soft.

Croydon

There was an old vicar of Croydon,
Whose cook was a regular hoyden.
She would sit on his knees,
While shelling the peas,
Or similar duties employed on.

Crumm

A frantic young woman named Crumm
Thought her lover too naïf and dumb.
She gave him no rest
'Til he straddled her chest,
And then she was all overcome.

Crumm

Said an innocent bowler named Crumm,
While massaging his fiancée's bum,
"My fingers, I know,
Are where they should go . . .
But what has become of my thumb?"

Cruze

A crusading lady named Cruze
Was highly advanced in her views.
She once in a zoo
Liberated a gnu,
And was lavishly praised by the *News*.

cry

Despite Betty Friedan's fierce cry,
There are some rights we men must deny.
I think you'll allow, sirs,
That feminine trousers
Need not be equipped with a fly.

Dahlia

There was a young lady named Dahlia
Whose bust was, in truth, utter failure.
She was surgically blessed
With a chest like Mae West,
And died happy of hypermammalia.

Dallas

A team playing baseball in Dallas
Called the umpire a shit out of malice.
While this worthy had fits,
The team made eight hits
And a girl in the bleachers named Alice.

Darjeeling

A surgical nurse in Darjeeling
Transplanted a prick to the ceiling.
When she wanted to ball,
It was no good at all,
But the dangle, she felt, was appealing.

Dave

There was a young fellow named Dave,
Who kept a dead whore in a cave.
He said, "I'll admit
I'm a bit of a shit,
But think of the money I save."

de Bray

On a weekend with Countess de Bray,
We beguiled a most tedious day
By sketching a penis
On a Titian Venus,
And a beard on a nude by Monet.

Dee

A cute London feminist, Dee,
Declared it was no longer free.
First, she got a whole crown,
Then her prices went down.
So did she.

Del Norte

There was a young wench in Del Norte,
Who liked to screw men over forty.
She said, "It's too quick
With a young feller's prick;
I like it to last and be warty."

deplorable

A virgin, whose tightness deplorable
Made regular sex seem too horrible,
At last had to marry
A dirty old fairy
Who thought her behind was adorable.

Deposit

Cohn said to his wife in Deposit,
"Tillie, now tell me, howzit
When we get into bed
You look over my head
And wink at the man in the closet?"

Des Moines

There was a young girl from Des Moines
Who was fond of rotating her loins.
She would take on a mate
For a very low rate,
Like a dime, or still smaller coins.

detective

To his bride said the lynx-eyed detective,
"Can it be that my eyesight's defective?
Has the east tit the least bit
The best of the west tit,
Or is it the faulty perspective?"

Detroit

There was a young girl from Detroit
Who at fucking was very adroit.
She'd contract her vagina
To a pinpoint or finer,
Or make it as big as a quoit.

The girl had a friend named Durand,
Whose cock could contract or expand.
He could bugger a midge,
Or the arch of a bridge;
Their performance together was grand.

Devizes

There was a young man of Devizes
Whose balls were of different sizes.
One was so small
It was nothing at all;
The other took numerous prizes.

Devon

There was a young lady from Devon
Attacked in a thicket by seven
Anglican priests—
Libidinous beasts—
Of such is the kingdom of heaven.

Dice

There was a young fellow from Dice,
Who remarked, "I think bigamy's nice.
Even two are a bore;
I'd prefer three or four,
For the plural of spouse . . . it is spice."

Dijon

There is an old harlot of Dijon,
Who in her old age got religion.
"When I'm dead and gone,"
She said, "I'll take on
The Father, the Son, and the Pigeon."

discard

Up in Cambridge, Lib 'Cliffies discard
Any pretense of being on guard.
Though the Harvards deny it,
Their saltpeter diet
Makes it hard to get hard in the Yard.

Don Quixote

Raise sabres! Salute Don Quixote!
Whose instincts were raunchy and goaty.
As his personal lance
Penetrated a nance,
He explained, "I don't normally go in for this
sort of thing, leaning strongly as I do
toward hetero rather than homo in all
matters pertaining to delights of the flesh...
But, you see, I was high on peyote!"

doom

Possessed by the devils of doom,
He made love to a ghost in a tomb.
He did it, they say,
In the regular way—
Under the sheets, I presume.

Doris

A comely young cave girl named Doris
Was raped by a male brontosaurus.
She exclaimed, "For a word
To explain what occurred,
I'd have to consult my thesaurus."

Dot

Said a civil rights worker named Dot,
"There's one thing I protesteth not:
When I lie in the street,
I think it's real neat
To be carried off showing my twat."

Dow

There was an old farmer named Dow,
Who said, "I feel wonderful now;
They've transplanted the tongue
And a piece of the lung,
And the liver which came from
mmmmmmmmmmmmy cow."

Doyle

A hot-blooded swordsman named Doyle
Didn't fence quite according to Hoyle.
When challenged to duel,
He would whip out his tool,
Which he brandished about like a foil.

Drake University

Said a coed from Drake University,
When asked about sexual diversity,
"While a lay is O.K.
In the regular way,
I *prefer* polymorphous perversity."

dream

Sheba's queen was King Solomon's dream,
Though their love life was not what 'twould se
For in those olden days
They had no scented sprays,
And she smelled like the Yale football team.

droll

A girl for a caddy is droll;
After golf, you may give her a roll.
But by night, as by day,
She is likely to say,
"You are playing, sir, the wrong hole."

dud

A hot roast often ends as a dud,
And it tastes like a goulash of crud.
In chef's cap or capote,
For a great table d'hôte,
The gourmet serves pressed duck *In Cold Blooc*

Duluth

A quick-trigger boy from Duluth
Was phoning his sweetheart named Ruth.
When he got his connection
He had an erection
And blew off all over the booth.

Duluth

There was an old maid of Duluth,
Who wept when she thought of her youth,
Remembering chances
She missed at school dances,
And once in a telephone booth.

Dundee

(To Winston Churchill)

A young man once went to Dundee,
And said to the voters, said he,
"No house is complete
Unless I have a seat;
My initials are W. C."

Dundee

There was an old man of Dundee,
Who came home as drunk as could be.
He wound up the clock
With the end of his cock,
And buggered his wife with the key.

Dunellen

The rosy-cheeked lass from Dunellen,
Whom the Hoboken sailors call Helen,
In her efforts to please,
Spread a social disease
From New York to the Straits of Magellan.

Durango

An ignorant maid of Durango
Wasn't told where to make a man's wang go,
But she added this knowledge
The first night in college,
With a sigh you could play as a tango.

Dutton

There was a young fellow named Dutton,
Whose balls were the size of a button,
But he had a dong
Some ten inches long,
But what could he do with it? Nuttin'.

East Bainbridge Hall

A student of East Bainbridge Hall
Had an organ exceedingly small.
He buggered a bug
On the edge of a rug,
But the bug didn't feel it at all.

East Birmingham

Lady Eva of East Birmingham
Got herself in a terrible jam.
While out on a bust,
She put too much trust
In the fit of a friend's diaphragm.

East Lynne

There was a young girl of East Lynne
Whose mother, to save her from sin,
Had filled up her crack
To the brim with shellac,
But the boys picked it out with a pin.

Eindhoven

At a concert one night in Eindhoven,
A virgin was raped to Beethoven.
As he kept to the beat,
She took note that his feet
Had no shoes, and no socks, and were cloven.

Elias

There was a young girl named Elias,
Whose panties were cut on the bias.
There was also a loop,
Through which she could poop,
And through which she'd been had once or twic

Ellis

A horny marine, Sergeant Ellis,
With esprit de corps much too zealous,
Drilled his yard to stand stiff
At the whiff of a quiff,
While his bottom blew *Semper Fidelis.*

emporium

The new cinematic emporium
Is by no means the merest sexorium,
But a highly effectual,
Heterosexual,
Mutual masturbatorium.

Erskine

There was a young lady of Erskine,
Who had a remarkable ferskine.
When I said to her, "Mabel,
You look fine in your sable,"
She replied, "I look best in my berskine."

Eton

There was a young lady of Eton,
Whose bottom had plenty of meat on.
She said, "Marry me, Jack,
And you'll find that my back-
Side's a nice place to warm your cold feet on."

Eutoxeter

There was a young girl from Eutoxeter,
And all the boys pushed their cocks at her.
From one of the cocks
She contracted the pox,
And poxed all the cocks in Eutoxeter.

Eva

There was a young lady named Eva,
Who went to a dance as Godiva,
But a change in the lights
Showed a rent in her tights;
A gentleman present cried, "Beaver!"

Exeter

There was a young lady of Exeter,
So pretty that men craned their necks at her.
One was even so brave
As to take out and wave
The distinguishing mark of his sex at her.

farm

A girl who came East from the farm
Exclaimed, "City life has its charm.
Take the pleasures of orgasm,
Ev'ry girl in New York has 'em,
But in Kansas they're viewed with alarm."

fashion

There was a young lady of fashion,
Who had oodles and oodles of passion.
To her lover she said,
As they piled into bed,
"This is one thing those bastards can't ration."

Faye

A lady biologist, Faye,
Hopes that parthenogenesis may
Some day sever the nexus
Between the two sexes.
How I hope I can live 'til that day!

fear

A man with venereal fear
Had intercourse in his wife's ear.
She said, "I don't mind,
Except that I find
When the telephone rings, I don't hear."

fête

At a rather too elegant fête,
Where a large group of dykes arrived late,
A cunnilingulate whore
And a queer from Mysore
Were engaged in bizarre tête-à-tête.

Fife

A mortician who practiced in Fife
Made love to the corpse of his wife.
"How would I know, Judge?
She was cold, did not budge—
Just the same as she'd acted in life."

fine

While computer advances are fine,
I am worried about their design.
When we link two machines,
Should we say that it means
They're engaged in a 360/9?

flock

After scolding his penitent flock,
The pontiff exhorted his cock,
"You pendulous shrimp,
You just dangle there limp;
You're supposed to be Peter, a Rock."

Florence

There was a young woman of Florence,
Who was looked on with general abhorrence.
In an amorous crush
Her bladder would flush,
And the stuff would come out in great torrents.

Florida

There was a young man from Florida
Who coveted a friend's wife and he
borrowed her.
When she opened her thighs,
He exclaimed in surprise,
"Why, that's not a cunt; it's a corridor."

Florida Keys

Said a man from the Florida Keys,
"We'll solve water pollution with ease.
Only wide constipation
Can now save the nation,
We must all live on alum and cheese."

flute

A tutor who tooted the flute
Tried to tutor two tutors to toot.
Said the two to the tutor,
"Is it harder to toot, or
To tutor two tutors to toot?"

Flynn

There was a young lady named Flynn,
Who thought fornication a sin,
But when she was tight
It seemed quite all right,
So everyone filled her with gin.

Formia

There was a young lady of Formia
Whose housekeeping ways would disarm ya.
When there came a cold snap,
She'd climb in your lap,
So her little base-burner could warm ya.

Fort Knapp

There was a young man from Fort Knapp
Who boasted a cock full of sap.
He said, with a snigger,
"It gets bigger and bigger,
Or, Christ, is it only the clap?"

frail

On the breast of a fair young frail
Was tattooed the price of her tail,
While on her behind,
For the sake of the blind,
Was the very same thing, but in Braille.

Fralee

There was a young girl from Fralee
Who was had by an ape in a tree.
The offspring was horrid,
All ass and no forehead,
Three balls, and a purple goatee.

France

An exchange U.S. student in France
Let Frenchmen galore in her pants.
"At home," she once said,
"We do it in bed,
But here it's a matter of chance."

France

A pretty young maiden of France
Decided she'd just take a chance.
She let herself go
In the lap of her beau,
And now all her sisters are aunts.

France

A Vassar girl over from France
Had a lover with St. Vitus dance.
This was awkward, they say,
At a meal or a play,
But was grand when he got in her pants.

France

(A rare three-liner)

There was a young fellow from France
Who waited ten years for his chance.
Then he muffed it.

Frei

Said an aged Madrid cocksman named Frei,
"I refuse these new fashions to try.
Why, every zipper
Is just Jack the Ripper!
I shall stick to my old Spanish fly."

frightful

The harlots in London are frightful,
And the fairies—the bastards—are spiteful,
But I'm not in a heat,
For I happened to meet
A sheep in Hyde Park. 'Twas delightful.

gall

A disqualified wrestler with gall,
As a woman had fooled one and all.
Said she, with a scream,
"I'd have made the men's team,
If they'd only transplanted one ball."

Gambetta

A president called Gambetta
Once used an imperfect French letter;
This was not the worst,
With disease he got cursed,
And he took a long time to get better.

Gates

There was a young sailor named Gates,
Who got along well with his mates,
'Til he fell on a cutlass,
Which rendered him buttless,
And practically useless on dates.

gay

There once was a pope who was gay;
He would ride down the Appian Way
And wink at the ladies
From his little Mercedes,
Which he'd nicknamed his *auto da fé.*

gender

"I should like," said my aunt, "to change gender.
Every part of me's bruised, torn, and tender,
For me man weighs a ton,
Six times nightly has fun,
And in short is a damned heavy spender."

Genoa

There was a young man from Genoa,
Whose prick was two inches, no moa.
It was all right for keyholes,
And little girls' pee-holes,
But quite out of place in a whoa.

Ghent

There was a young fellow from Ghent,
Whose cock was so long that it bent.
To save himself trouble,
He put it in double,
And instead of coming, he went!

Gherrity

There was a young widow named Gherrity,
Who said, with a mordant asperity,
"I'd have cut off his dilly
To use occasionally,
Had he not willed the thing to a charity."

gingery

A young lad with passions quite gingery
Tore a hole in his sister's best lingerie.
He pinched her behind,
And made up his mind
To add incest to insult and injury.

Giotto

An Italian painter named Giotto
Seduced a nun in a grotto.
The result of his crime
Was two boys at one time;
"Give your sons to the church," was his motto.

Glaze

A Cordon Bleu *Charlotte* named *Glaze*
Makes *hors d'oeuvres* which truly a*maize.*
The men in her classes
Not only make passes,
She gives them all straight *bordelaise.*

Glengarry

There was a young man of Glengarry,
Whose cock was too heavy to carry.
So he put it on wheels
And hired trained seals
For his opening night in Wilkes-Barre.

Gloria

There was a young lady named Gloria,
Who was had by Sir Gerald du Maurier,
And then by six men,
Sir Gerald again,
And the band at the Waldorf Astoria.

Gloucester

There was a young girl from Gloucester
Whose parents thought they had lost her.
But they found in the grass
The marks of her ass
And the knees of the man who had crossed her.

glum

As an athlete my future was glum;
I was cursed with a too active bum.
Said my doc, "For your Wheaties,
Substitute cantharides,
Then, instead of going, you'll come."

Gore

Theological student Tom Gore,
While using his fist for a whore,
Said, "It's not a solution
For total pollution,
But I can always come back for more."

Goring

There was a young person of Goring,
Who made a small hole in the flooring.
He lined it all round,
Then laid on the ground,
And declared it was cheaper than whoring.

Gossal

A young geologist from Gossal
Discovered a fossil colossal.
He could tell by the bend,
And the knob on the end,
'Twas the peter of Paul the Apostle.

Gotch

Great woe befell Bernadine Gotch,
While camped by Franconia Notch.
She was raped by an eagle,
Or maybe a sea gull,
Which then built a nest in her crotch.

Grace

A Bennington student named Grace
Slipped a barbed-wire pessary in place.
Her Chinese professor
Bent down to caress her,
And moaned through cut lips, "I rooz face."

grace

In the midst of an anthem of grace,
The choirmaster slipped from his place
To goose the soprano
In a lingering manner,
And return with a smile on his face.

Grant

There was a young fellow named Grant,
Who was built like a sensitive plant.
When asked, "Do you fuck?"
He replied, "No such luck;
I would if I could but I can't."

Greece

That naughty old Sappho of Greece
Said, "What I prefer to a piece
Is to have my pudenda
Rubbed hard by the enda
The little pink nose of my niece."

Greely

A free-lancing artist named Greely
Had a model that suited ideally.
At the first scent of paint,
She would fall in a faint,
And only revived when lanced freely.

Green

There was a young lady named Green,
Who grew so abnormally lean,
And flat, and compressed,
That her back touched her chest,
And sideways she couldn't be seen.

Green Bay

A tackle who played for Green Bay
Was in training each night and each day.
Isometric coition
May improve one's condition,
But it isn't as much fun that way.

Greenwich

There was a young fellow from Greenwich
Who lived on nothing but speenwich.
It lengthened his tool,
Which he kept on a spool,
And unwound it, eenwich by eenwich.

Gression

A big-bosomed Bunny named Gression
Sold cigars at a Key Club concession.
When she swiveled about,
Even strong men cried out,
For her costume did not keep her flesh in.

Grimes

There was a young lady named Grimes,
Who spent all her nickels and dimes
On satin and lace
To hold her in place
And keep her abreast of the times.

grouch

Winter is here with its grouch;
The time when you sneeze and you slouch,
And you can't go canoeing
To get in your screwing,
But a lot can be done on a couch.

hack

There once was a lexicon hack
Whose alphabet knowledge was slack.
'Stead of *aardvark* to *zygote,*
Finishing the Os, he got
Up to P, and he never came back.

halting

In Sodom, great feasts knew no halting,
And Lot was the guest they all called in.
Said each host, "We love you,
But your wife must come, too;
The stew is too flat and needs salting."

Handel

There was a musician named Handel
Whose intimate life was a scandal.
When he fugued his bass
He grew red in the face
And buggered himself with a candle.

hang

Dear ladies, we don't give a hang
If you start up a feminine gang.
But here is the thing:
If you don't have our ying,
What the heck will you do with your yang?

Hannah

A prissy old maid named Miss Hannah
Wrote Burbank a note in this manner:
Could you spare a few hours
From your shrubs and your flowers
And put a pulse in the banana?

Hannibal

In the land where once ruled old Hannibal
There's an evening quite easily plannable:
Ten blacks in a row,
And all of them blow,
But one of the ten is a cannibal.

Hare

A very young surgeon named Hare
Told *Time* what he'd done on a dare.
"I gave a lobotomy
To twin hippopotami.
Now one of them's running for mayor."

Harridge

There was a young lady of Harridge,
Who said, on the morn of her marriage,
"I shall sew my chemise
Right down to my knees;
I refuse to be fucked in the carriage."

Harriet

There was a young lady named Harriet
Who dreamt she'd been raped in a chariot
By the Man in the Moon,
Sir Philip Sassoon,
Biff Crosby, and Judas Iscariot.

Harrow

A hopeful young fellow from Harrow
Once feathered his cock like an arrow.
"There's room for improvement,"
Said his girl, "in the movement.
Make it flutter about like a sparrow."

Harrow

There was a young lady of Harrow
Who complained that her cunt was too narrow.
For times without number
She would use a cucumber,
But could not accomplish a marrow.

Harwich

There was a young person of Harwich,
Tried to grind his betrothed in a carriage.
She said, "No, you young goose;
Just try self-abuse,
And the other we'll try after marriage."

Hasdrubable

There was a young man named Hasdrubable,
Who had one real and one rubber ball.
Not to be out-witted,
His wife was two-teated;
She had one rubber bub and one rubbable.

Hatch

There once was a young man named Hatch
Who thought that he'd made a great catch.
His inducement to flirt
Was a wee mini-skirt,
But, alas, she'd a wee mini-snatch.

Hatch

There was a young lady named Hatch
Who had a rectangular snatch,
So she practiced coition
With a mathematician
Who had a square root to match.

Hatch

There was a young lady named Hatch,
Who said, "I just adore Bach;
He isn't so fussy
As Brahms or Debussy;
Sit down, and I'll play you a snatch."

Havana

A deep baritone from Havana,
While singing, slipped on a banana.
He was ill for a year,
Then resumed his career
As a promising lyric soprano.

Hayes

A patient young Girl Scout named Hayes
Rubbed two fagots together for days,
'Til she happened to pass
A portion of gas,
Which kindled a wonderful blaze.

he

So dextrous a doctor was he,
His technique was something to see.
'Til nurse Dowd, a virgin,
Cried out, "Oh, my surgeon!
You poked the wrong organ in me!"

Hearst

A notorious whore named Miss Hearst
In the pleasures of men is well versed.
Reads a sign o'er the head
Of her well-rumpled bed:
The customer always comes first!

Helen

The breasts of a woman named Helen
Were the size of a large watermelon.
When she hove into sight,
All the men would take fright
And run away, screamin' and yellin'.

hernia

There was a young girl with the hernia,
Who said to her doctor, "Gol dern ya!
When slicing my middle,
I pray do not fiddle
With matters that do not concern ya."

hero

For the next Games' finale, the hero
Gets a crack at the empress's zero,
While the emperor stands by
Swinging out *Träumerei*
On his flame-throwing fiddle.
Signed,
Nero.

hetera

A lady stockholder, quite hetera,
Decided her fortunes to bettera.
On the floor, quite unclad,
She successively had
Merrill Lynch, Pierce, Fenner, et cetera.

high

Said the truck driver, shifting to high,
And stroking his passenger's thigh,
"Inside my valise
Are some rubbers and grease;
Let's open them up, bye and bye."

Hilary

There was a young soldier named Hilary
Who spent sev'ral days in the pillory.
Reconnoit'ring a lass,
He had reached such a pass
That he brought up his heavy artillery.

Hilda

There was a young lady named Hilda
Who went for a walk with a builder.
He knew that he could,
And he should and he would;
And he did...and he goddamn near killed her.

hipped

A gal from L. A. who was hipped
Went out to the beach to get dipped.
She had on a Jantzen,
But only the pants, 'n
She found herself at Sunset, stripped.

Hitchin

There was a young fellow named Hitchin
Who was screwing the maid in the kitchen.
When his ass got too close to
The red-hot stove toaster,
He woke up the house with his bitchin'.

Hohokus

A cameraman from Hohokus
Tried to capture the mayor in focus.
It turned out a loss
For he pictured the boss
With six aldermen kissing his tokus.

Hollis

A hillbilly farmer named Hollis
Used possums and snakes for his solace.
The children had scales
And prehensile tails
And voted for Governor Wallace.

Hoople

There was a young maiden named Hoople
Whose bosom was triple, not duple.
She had one removed,
But it grew back, improved;
At present, Miss Hoople's quadruple.

Howard

Full of lust, a swim teacher, Bill Howard,
Was screwing a girl while she showered.
He told her, "I hope
You're still holding the soap,
Or else it's the Lux I've deflowered."

Huan

A wise Chinese druggist named Huan
Was awarded a prize by the khan
For a sexual depressive
To calm thoughts obsessive;
It is now known as Upjohn's *Down John.*

Hugh

A stalwart young Klansman named Hugh
Once dreamed he turned into a Jew.
He woke with a shock
And looked at his cock
And found it was perfectly true.

Hughes

There was an old fellow named Hughes,
Who swore off on all kinds of booze.
Said he, "When I'm muddled,
My senses get fuddled,
And I pass up too damn many screws."

Hyde

Said ex-Bunny, Miss Winifred Hyde,
"I, the person, will not be denied."
When asked, "What's to be done,
When a man wants his fun?"
"You can play with yourselves," she replied.

illusion

Said a Spaniard, with little illusion,
As he felt on his head a contusion,
"The thugs from South Spain
Are not only a pain,
They are also a snare Andalusian."

imperfections

A real-estate man's imperfections
As a lover caused female rejections.
"I'm deflated," he moaned,
"They're erogenous-zoned,
But only for high-rise erections."

Iraq

There was a young man from Iraq,
Who played the bass viol with his cock.
With tremendous erections,
He rendered selections
From Johann Sebastian Bach.

Isthmus

There was a young man from the Isthmus
Whose bride had acute vaginismus.
They found themselves stuck
On the very first fuck,
And had to stay that way 'til Christmas.

Jacques

A painter of Pop, known as Jacques,
Intends each new canvas to shock.
Outsized genitalia
Gave the critics heart-failia,
But one dubbed it pure Poppycock.

jam

On the ark there was soon a great jam,
So Noah ate much veal and young lamb.
But the taboos on pig
Made that meat *infra dig,*
Though in secret Noah sometimes ate Ham.

Janus

A noted torero named Janus
Was censored for conduct quite heinous.
He was told, "On the bull
Use your sword, *not* your tool,
And aim for the neck, not the anus."

Japan

The ladies who live in Japan
Exist just for pleasing a man.
They'll give him fellatio,
Or a lay on the patio,
Or even a goose with a fan.

Japan

There was a young man of Japan
Whose limericks never would scan.
When someone asked why,
He would slowly reply,
"Perhaps it's because I always try to get as
many dirty words in
the last line as I possibly can."

There was a young fellow from China
Whose sense of verse was much finer.
He thought it divine
To end the last line
Quite suddenly.

Joan

There was a young lady named Joan
Who got all her thrills from the phone,
Secreting the bell,
And receiver as well,
Where you wouldn't believe, if not shown.

Jude

There once was a lady named Jude
Who was such an impeccable prude
That she pulled down the blind
When changing her mind,
Lest a curious eye should intrude.

Kannel

When they probed a young woman named
Kannel,
Who complained she felt choked in her channel,
They found shoehorns and spoons,
Several busted balloons,
And twenty-two yards of red flannel.

Kate

A beautiful maiden named Kate
Reclined in the dark with her date.
When asked how she fared,
She said she was scared,
But otherwise doing first-rate.

Kay

A militant teenager, Kay,
Joined a protest one cold winter's day.
She ignited her bra,
But—ha-ha-ha-ha!—
There's no heat in a 28A.

Kay

Ephraim and his crusading Kay
Love to picket by night and by day.
They walk the same line
And hold up a sign,
Which shows where you see Eph you see Kay.

Keating

There was a young fellow of Keating,
Whose pride took a terrible beating.
That happens to males
When they learn the details
Of their wives' extramarital cheating.

Kelly

There was a young couple named Kelly,
Who were stuck tight, belly to belly.
It seemed, in their haste,
They'd used Library Paste,
Instead of Petroleum Jelly.

Kent

There was a young lady from Kent
Who said that she knew what it meant
When he asked her to dine—
Private room, lots of wine—
She knew, oh, she knew! But she went.

Kent

Three elderly spinsters of Kent
Gave up copulation for Lent.
This included door handles,
Both tapers and candles,
And anything else that was bent.

Kew

A hermaphrodite fairy of Kew
Offered boys something new in a screw.
They both looked so sweet
On the front and back seat
Of a bisexual built just for two.

Kew

Said a lusty young maiden of Kew,
"I don't smoke, I don't drink, I don't chew.
But do not think, therefore,
There's nothing I care for,
If you know what I mean . . . and you do."

Kew

There was a young lady of Kew
Who said, as the curate withdrew,
"I prefer the dear vicar;
He's longer and thicker.
Besides, he comes quicker than you."

Khartoum

A pansy who lived in Khartoum
Took a lesbian up to his room.
And they argued all night
Over who had the right
To do what, and with which, and to whom.

Khartoum

There was an old man of Khartoum,
Who kept a small goat in his room.
"It reminds me," he said,
"Of a lady who's dead,
But I cannot remember of whom."

Khief

There was an old abbot of Khief,
Who thought the Impenitent Thief
Had ballocks of brass
And an amethyst ass;
He died in this awful belief.

Kildare

There was a young man from Kildare
Who was having a girl in a chair.
At the sixty-third stroke,
The furniture broke,
And his rifle went off in the air.

Kilkenny

There was an old girl of Kilkenny
Whose usual charge was a penny.
For the half of that sum
You could roger her bum—
A source of amusement to many.

king

The last time I dined with the king,
He did a remarkable thing;
As he sat on the stool
And fondled his tool,
He remarked, "If I play, will you sing?"

King's

There was a young fellow of King's,
Who was weary of women and things.
Said he, "My desire
Is a boy from the choir,
With an ass that's like Jell-O on springs."

King's Bluff

There was an old whore of King's Bluff,
Who said, "I have had quite enough
Of men who are thirty,
And forty and fifty;
What I need is that greasy kid stuff."

Kip

An obese old broker named Kip
Took a very fat girl on a trip.
He was talking of stock,
As he put in his cock.
At the end, she said, "Thanks for the tip."

knew

An anonymous woman we knew
Was dozing one day in her pew.
When the preacher yelled, "Sin!"
She said, "Count me in,
As soon as the service is through."

Kress

For his concert, a flautist named Kress
Was in such a great hurry to dress,
That on a high run
His fly came undone,
And his organ got raves from the Press.

Kroch

A cheerful young golfer named Kroch
Gave his tee shot a hundred-yard sock.
It doesn't sound far
For the man who shoots par,
But 'twas done with the end of his cock.

Kroll

A corpulent maiden named Kroll
Had a notion exceedingly droll;
At a masquerade ball,
Dressed in nothing at all,
She backed in as a Parker House roll.

kvetch

A harlot who was an old kvetch
Came nine times with a well-endowed wretch.
Then, with prick 'twixt her thighs,
She declared between sighs,
"I'd call this the tenth-inning stretch."

Lady Norris

"'Tis my custom," said dear Lady Norris,
"To beg lifts from the drivers of lorries.
When they get out to piss,
I see things that I miss
At the wheel of my two-seater Morris."

La Jolla

There is an old man of La Jolla,
With a habit that's sure to anolla.
Before telling a joke,
He'll give you a poke,
And remark, "This will really destrolla."

Lake

Said a lovely young maiden named Lake,
Most pervertedly fond of a snake,
"If my good friend, the boa,
Shoots spermatozoa,
What offspring we'll leave in our wake."

Lamar

There's a buxom young wench in Lamar,
Whose shape is too nubile by far.
One luscious bazoom
Fills up half the room,
And you couldn't go round her in par.

Lancelot

There was a young fellow named Lancelot
Whom the neighbors all looked at askance a lot
For whenever he'd pass
A presentable lass,
The front of his pants would advance a lot.

land

Moaned Tessie, the whore, "In this land,
I've met bastards who thought it was grand
To retire, when inclined,
With sex problems in mind,
And awake with solution in hand."

Lapp

There was a young lecher named Lapp
Who thought condoms were so much crap.
Said he, "All us he-men
Like to scatter our semen."
Ten weeks later he still has the clap.

larks

Said a lassie on one of her larks,
"It's more fun indoors than in parks.
You feel more at ease,
Your ass doesn't freeze,
And strollers don't make snide remarks."

Lars

In Rome, a curator called Lars
Found, preserved in a cache of old jars,
The cunny of Venus,
Old Jupiter's penis,
And, he *thinks,* the left knocker of Mars.

lass

There was an eccentric young lass
Who wore panties constructed of brass.
Said she, "They have uses,
Like staving off gooses,
And pinches and pins in the ass."

last

An emasculate lad said, "At last,
I've an elephant trunk for a mast.
Though usually great,
I do have to state
I'm embarrassed when peanuts are passed."

La Verne

There was a young bride named La Verne,
Who found she'd a great deal to learn.
The man she had wed
Took young boys into bed,
And she didn't know which way to turn.

lay

There was a young woman who lay
With her legs wide apart in the hay.
Then calling a ploughman,
She said, "Do it now, man!
Don't wait 'til your hair has turned gray."

lea

All the streams that water the lea
Are quite pestilential with pee.
But the gallons of sperm
Spread nary a germ;
In rubber they float to the sea.

Lear

There was an old farmer named Lear
Who possessed a fine cow that gave beer.
Budweiser and Schlitz
Could be tapped from her tits,
And pretzels came out of the rear.

Lee

A Quaker bartender named Lee
Avoided all raucous melee,
But got up his ire
At religious inquire,
And quietly murmured, "Fuck thee!"

Lee

I dined with the duchess of Lee,
Who asked, "Do you fart when you pee?"
I replied, with some wit,
"Do you belch when you shit?"
And felt it was one up to me.

Leeds

There once was a farmer of Leeds
Who swallowed a packet of seeds.
When the first week was over,
He sprouted in clover,
And couldn't sit down for the weeds.

Leeds

There once was a lecher of Leeds
Who did up his privates in tweeds,
With a zipper installed,
To keep them close-hauled,
Or released for his amorous needs.

Leeman

A curvaceous young lady named Leeman
Refused naval dates with much screamin'.
It was not that the army
Was any more charmy,
But the gal was allergic to seamen.

Leigh

There was a young plumber of Leigh,
Who was plumbing a gal by the sea.
She said, "Stop your plumbing,
There's somebody coming."
Said the plumber, still plumbing, "It's me."

Leo

A cowboy, by birthright a Leo,
Once met a young lady in Rio.
A full night and day
They spent in the hay,
And now the poor cowboy can't pee-o.

Leon

At Mills, a professor named Leon
Taught heresies most Manichean.
Quoth the girls, "Though it's pleasant,
Let's disdain this crude peasant;
Or, as Mexicans say, 'Peon Leon!' "

Lessing

There was a young lady from Lessing,
Whose cock-eating ways were distressing.
She would insert the head,
'Twixt two slices of bread,
And munch it without even dressing.

Levine

A seamstress named Bertha Levine
Caught her breast in her sewing machine.
She saw, with a shudder,
That stitched on her udder
Was "God Bless Our Home," done in green.

Libra

A lady philologist (Libra)
Was raped by an oversexed zebra.
She cried out her anguish
In every known languish,
Including Swahili and Hebra.

life

Joseph led a real gourmet's life
(Though he always ate pulse with his knife).
When the cook cried out, "Sir!
Try this great *pot au feu,"*
Old Joseph tried Potiphar's wife.

Liliom

To her gardener a lady named Liliom
Said, "Billy, plant roses and trillium."
Then she started to fool
With the gardener's tool,
And wound up in the bed of sweet William.

limbo

As he struggled to heaven from limbo,
Dante murmured to Beatrice, his bimbo,
"Sure, you want to scrimmage,
But think of my image;
Don't lie with your pussy akimbo."

limousine

An astronomer's swift limousine
Went through a red light in Racine.
He was going so fast
That the light which he passed,
Through Doppler effect, showed as green.

Lionheart

King Richard was called Lionheart
But he fell for a sixpenny tart.
The girl herself said,
When he crawled in her bed,
That the best he could do was to fart.

Loch Ness

There was a young man from Loch Ness,
Whose sexual life was a mess,
'Til the beast in the Loch
Bit the head off his cock,
Which solved all his problems, I guess!

Lodge

A cautious young fellow named Lodge
Had seat belts installed in his Dodge.
When his date was strapped in,
He committed a sin,
Without even leaving the g'rage.

Lolita

A twelve-year-old nymphet, Lolita,
Was expert at eating a peter.
She demurely would say,
"I shall chew it all day;
I'm a slow but fastidious eater."

look

Abou asked, as he sneaked a quick look,
"What you writin' in that big gold book?"
The angel screamed, "Ben!
You ask once again,
And I'll take your name off the list, schnook."

Loont

A Lancashire 'ore named Loont
'Ad a clevah promotional stoont.
When the hayer was so foul
You coont see at oul,
She burned a red flayer in her coont.

Loretta

A lonely old maid named Loretta
Sent herself an anonymous letter,
Quoting Ellis on sex,
And *Oedipus Rex,*
And exclaimed, "I already feel better."

Loretta

A toothsome young lass named Loretta
Had good reasons for wearing a sweater.
Of the three that she had,
Keeping warm was not bad;
The two others were visibly better.

Louth

There was a young lady of Louth,
Who returned from a trip in the South.
Her father said, "Nelly,
There's more in your belly
Than ever went in at your mouth."

lugger

There was a young mate of a lugger,
Who took out a girl, just to hug her.
"I've my monthlies," she said,
"And a cold in my head,
But my bowels are all right. Do you bugger?"

Lundy

There was an old parson of Lundy,
Fell asleep in the vestry on Sunday.
He awoke with a scream,
"What! Another wet dream?
That comes of not frigging since Monday."

Lupescu

The beautiful Madame Lupescu
Once came to Rumania's rescue.
It's a very fine thing
To be under a king;
Is democracy better? I esk you.

Lyme

There was a young fellow from Lyme
Who married three wives at one time.
When asked, "Why the third?"
He replied, "One's absurd,
And bigamy, sir, is a crime!"

Lynn

There was a young fellow from Lynn,
Whose cock was the size of a pin.
Said his girl, with a laugh,
As she fondled his staff,
"Well, this won't be much of a sin."

MacFooshan

There once was a Scot named MacFooshan
Whose tool had an odd convolution,
And filled him with guilt,
For the tilt of his kilt
Caused frequent diurnal pollution.

Madder

A nude Negro model, Rose Madder,
Took refuge beneath a high ladder.
But the sculptor, Brancusi,
Unafraid of black pussy,
Walked under the ladder and had her.

madder

As Titian was mixing rose madder,
His model ascended the ladder.
Her position to Titian
Suggested coition,
So he mounted the ladder and had her.

Madras

There was a young maid from Madras
Who had a magnificent ass,
Not rounded and pink,
As you probably think,
It was gray, had long ears, and ate grass.

Madras

There was a young man of Madras
Who was having a boy in the grass.
Then a cobra de capello
Said, "Hello, young fellow!"
And bit a piece out of *his* ass.

Madrid

An unfortunate man from Madrid
Had both Superego and Id.
So whether he screwed
Or entirely eschewed,
He suffered, whatever he did.

Madrid

There was an old man of Madrid,
Who cast loving eyes on a kid.
He said, "Oh, my joy!
I shall bugger that boy.
You see if I don't" . . . and he did.

Madrid

There was a young girl from Madrid,
Who said she had never been rid.
There came an Italian,
With balls like a stallion,
Who said that he would . . . and he did.

Maguire

A quishykirk queer named Maguire
Hung a sign out *"Asshole for Hire.*
You can buy by the piece
Or on quarterly lease;
For clerical rates, please enquire."

Mahler

A German musician named Mahler
Had his balls insured for a dollar.
One ball was petite,
Like a wee grain of wheat;
The other, considerably smaller.

mahout

There was an old Hindu mahout
Who said, "What's all this blithering about?
Why, I have shot spunk
Up an elephant's trunk."
Cries of "Shame!" "Kick his ass!" "Throw
him out!"

maid

Joan of Arc was renowned as a maid;
That means she had never been laid.
She wore iron britches
With stainless steel stitches,
Which is why she was never afraid.

Maine

There was a young lady from Maine
Whose face was exceedingly plain,
But her cunt had a pucker
That made the men fuck her
Again and again and again.

male

Mercurians, female and male,
Whenever they tear off some tail,
Do all of their lovin'
Inside of an oven,
And think of us Earthlings as frail.

Maloff

Said a famous French chef, Jean Maloff,
"Though my omelets are tiny and tough,
Let the customers beg
For more than one egg;
For a Frenchman, one egg is un oeuf."

Malotte

Said a zookeeper's wife named Malotte,
As she stuffed some live ants up her twat,
"Of all sexual sensations,
The eccentric gyrations
Of an anteater's tongue tops the lot."

man

Moses was a constipated man.
Once high up on Mt. Sinai he ran.
From a bush, the Lord hissed,
"I'll give you an assist;
Here's two tablets; they're called *Serutan*."

Manila

A Good Humor man from Manila
Stuck a freezer inside a gorilla
Which, when fed the right food
And benignantly screwed,
Shit chocolate, orange ice, and vanilla.

Mao

In the words of the good Chairman Mao,
"A woman is much like a cao."
Has he thereby admitted
Their girls are four-titted,
Or that heifers resemble his frao?

Marge

There was a young maiden named Marge,
Who swam in the nude from a barge.
'Til a man in a punt
Disappeared up her cunt,
An organ admittedly large.

Marine

There was a young Royal Marine
Whose musical ear was obscene.
He said, "Isn't it odd,
But I never know 'God
Save the Weasel' from 'Pop Goes the Queen.' "

marine

To his girl said a Cornish marine,
"You've the knobbiest coastline I've seen.
To put into port
Would be jolly good sport,
If the rest of the fleet hadn't been."

marks

If Leo your own birthday marks,
You'll have sex until forty, when starts
A new pleasure in stamps,
Boy Scouts, and their camps,
And fondling nude statues in parks.

Marrs

"I'll stand up for my rights," yelled Miss Marrs,
But all she could show were some scars.
For the males, as one, rose
And resorted to blows,
When she crashed homosexual bars.

Martell

There was a young man named Martell,
Who created the wildest cartel.
He bought up dead pricks
And rubbed them with Vicks
For sore throats . . . Oh, my God! How they sell

Martha

There was a young lady named Martha;
When the girls went far, she went fartha.
The affairs were good fun,
The result was a son,
Named Donohue, Smith, or McArtha.

masses

Young Joe is just one of the masses
Of guys quite adept with the lasses.
He remarked with some fright,
As he kissed her goodnight,
"Spread your legs, dear, you're breaking my
glasses."

mate

Now computers find fellows a mate;
A McLuhanish, digital fate.
When a child comes to pass,
He's tattooed on his ass:
"Do Not Staple, Bend, Fold, Mutilate."

Mather

On a heart transplant, patient Tom Mather
Worked himself into a lather.
Said he, "The idea's good,
But, God, if I could
Have a new prostate gland, I'd much rather."

May

A young airline stewardess, May,
Has achieved liberation today.
She screwed without quittin'
From New York to Britain;
It's clear she has come a long way.

Mays

A hungry young linguist named Mays
Played with a fruit salad for days.
"To hell with a cherry,
I seek a red berry,
If permitted to coign a *fraise*."

McBride

There was a young man named McBride,
Who fell in a privy and died.
The next day his brother
Fell into another,
And now they're interred, side by side.

McComb

There was an old maid named McComb
Who liked her men tall and handsome.
(She could also make do
With a finger or two,
Or the end of her calloused old thumb.)

McGee

"How I wonder," said Sarah McGee,
"Why my lover's lost interest in me;
Is it that I can't dance,
Or the lock on my pants
For which I won't give him the key?"

McGill

The dong of a dean of McGill
Was adorned with a porcupine quill.
"It looks odd," he agreed,
"But the thing's guaranteed
To provide an additional thrill."

McGuff

"Great God!" wailed Peter McGuff,
"What the hell is all of this stuff!
She twiddles my prick,
Gets it stiff as a stick,
Then denies me the use of her muff."

McGurk

There was a young man named McGurk
Who dozed off one night after work.
He had a wet dream,
But awoke with a scream,
Just in time to give it a jerk.

McHugh

There was a young man named McHugh,
Whose ideas were exciting and new,
But an ancient relation
Gave disapprobation
To McHugh spelling *fuq* (with a *q*).

McKesson

A curious old maid named McKesson
Walked in while a man was undressin'.
Said he with a sneer,
As he came in her ear,
"I guess that'll teach you a lesson."

McMitchin

There was a young girl named McMitchin
Who was scratching her twat in the kitchen.
Her mother said, "Rose,
It's crabs, I suppose?"
Rose said, "Yes, and, by Jesus, they're itchin'."

McNair

A balding young man named McNair
Patched his pate with the snatch of a bear.
Said he, "A shampoo
Is as good as a screw,
And I come when I'm combing my hair."

McNamiter

There was a young man named McNamiter
With a tool of prodigious diameter.
But it wasn't the size
Gave the girls a surprise,
But his rhythm . . . iambic pentameter.

McNary

Said his virginal bride to McNary,
"I've saved myself just for you, Harry."
But to his chagrin,
When he screwed his way in,
He found there were seeds in her cherry.

McNeff

The cross-eyed old painter, McNeff,
Was color-blind, palsied, and deaf.
When he asked to be touted,
The critics all shouted,
"This is art with a capital *f*!"

McPherson

A happy old hag named McPherson
Was really the *busiest* person;
Spent her days, for a fact,
In the sexual act,
And all of her nights in rehearsing.

McSidney

The great Glasgow surgeon, McSidney,
Was convinced if he transferred a kidney
From a whale to a conger
It would piss a lot longer.
He could not have been wronger. It didna.

McSwill

A cute dean of Women, McSwill,
Took the contraceptivity pill.
For a lovely semester
All men could molest her;
Her need for resistance was nil.

McWhinners

A divine by the name of McWhinners
Held classes each evening for sinners.
They were sectioned and graded
So the very degraded
Would not be held back by beginners.

McWilde

Said a man-hater, Willa McWilde,
"Godammit, I find I'm with child.
But the heart of the bother
Was telling the father;
The son-of-a-bitch only smiled!"

Medina

Mohammed, when lodged at
Medina,
Imported a fifth wife from China,
Being anxious to know
If it really were so
That their maids have a squinting vagina.

member

Being cursed with a very small member,
My friend Shorty Dunn must remember
To open his fly
On the Fourth of July,
In order to pee in September.

men

Brave Daniel was a man among men,
And for football he had a great yen.
He became so adroit
He was tapped by Detroit,
And was cast into the Lions' den.

men

Pass not this lonely grave by, men.
Pass not without a deep sigh, men.
For here lies Jane Jorgans,
With all her own organs,
Including, alas, her own hymen.

mention

A young man, whose name we won't mention,
Had a transplant to lower his tension.
At the beat of his heart,
He'd let out a fart,
And his penis would snap to attention.

Merton

There was a young fellow from Merton
Who went out with only his shirt on,
From which did peep shyly
His *membrum virile,*
For people to animadvert on.

Metuchen

A meticulous man from Metuchen
Had a small flea upon his escutcheon.
When asked, "Why the flea?"
He replied, "Well, you see,
There wasn't much room to put much in."

Milnocket

A curious lad in Milnocket
Went to bed with a solid-fuel rocket.
As he tossed in his sleep,
He ignited the heap;
Now he's worn by his girl in a locket.

miss

Once bedded, your militant miss
Is likely to say, with a hiss,
"By God, all us sisters
Would kick out you misters,
If we didn't need *that* to fit *this*."

miss

There was an aesthetic young miss
Who thought it the apex of bliss
To jazz herself silly
With the bud of a lily,
Then go to the garden and piss.

Mission

A certain young person of Mission,
In a sadly befuddled condition,
Confused picture and song
And declared to a throng
That *The Lady in Red* was by Titian.

mission

The Venusians, out on a mission,
Found Earth in a puzzling condition.
They could understand part
Of our laws and our art,
But got stuck in the fifteenth position.

Mithridates

Of that terrible King, Mithridates,
His subjects along the Euphrates
Used to say with great scorn,
"He's not of woman born,
But extruded from fatherly nates."

Mohican

I once knew a crazy Mohican
Who got all his jollies from peekin';
He liked to watch bears
Carry on their affairs,
And the rooster seducing the chicken.

Moll Flanders

Consider the life of Moll Flanders,
Which was spent among harlots and panders,
'Til that worn-out old bitch
Became suddenly rich
On a stock-market tip from Ann Landers.

molls

Whenever the Women's Lib molls
Throw parties, they tear down the walls;
They sing and they dance,
In their bell-bottom pants,
But you can't say they really have balls.

money

A man who came into some money
Decided to marry a Bunny,
But the thought of the ears
And the tails of the dears
Made him skip it as being too funny.

Montrose

There was an old whore in Montrose
Who'd go off any time that she chose.
She could do it, they say,
Ninety-nine times a day,
And if that is no record, it's close.

Montrose

There was a young lad from Montrose
Who could diddle himself with his toes.
He could do it so neat,
He fell in love with his feet,
And christened them Myrtle and Rose.

Moravia

There was a young girl of Moravia
Whose beauty would surely enslave ya,
While her double-knee action
Lent greater attraction
To her happy amoral behavior.

Morgan

A surgeon named Timothy Morgan
Was a whiz at transplanting an organ.
For twenty-five grand,
He'd install one goat gland,
One prick, and two balls . . . quite a bargain!

Mose

They stitched a new gland into Mose,
But some untoward symptoms arose;
When he fingered a quiff,
It made his ears stiff,
And he always would come through his nose.

Mose's wife cried, "I'd not give two pins
For our chances to breed kiths or kins!"
But Mose sank to his knees
And managed to sneeze,
And now he's the father of twins.

Moses

A religious young miner named Moses
Contracted pneumonoultramicroscopicsilicovol-
canoconiosis.
This, plus the schism
Between Mary Baker Eddy and antidisestablish-
mentarianism,
Made him feel supercalifragilisticexpialidocious.

mountain

There was an old man of the mountain,
Who frigged himself into a fountain.
Fifteen times had he spent,
Still he wasn't content;
He simply got tired of counting.

Myrtle

There was a young lady named Myrtle
Who had an affair with a turtle.
She had crabs, so they say,
In nine months and a day,
Which proves that the turtle was fertile.

Myrtle

This cute English lassie named Myrtle
Was so fecund and fruitful and fertile,
She was got with a child
By Sir Christopher Wilde
Through a crack in her chastity girdle.

mystery

The *Iliad's* really no mystery,
Though details are blustery and blistery.
It's a long story tellin'
Of the search for Queen Helen,
And the prize horse's ass in all history.

name

On Eros, despite its fair name,
The sexes are one and the same.
If amusing oneself
By abusing oneself
Leads to pregnancy, isn't life tame?

nation

Though each brave of the Cherokee
nation
May discover some baroque elation
In beating his prick
With a hickory stick,
I am sure it's a rare recreation.

nation

Though the virile young priests of the nat
Waited breathless throughout its gestation,
The bull of Pope Paul
Offered nothing at all,
Save prolonged and restrained celibation.

Nattick

There was a young lady from Nattick
Whose sex life was very erratic.
She dodged every feller,
From third floor to cellar,
But slept with them all in the attic.

neater

There never was anything neater
Than the bishop of Chichester's peter.
In the heat of a clinch
It would stretch from an inch
To just a bit short of a meter.

Nefertiti

The pussy of Queen Nefertiti
Was known to be quite itty-bitty,
'Til she got with great trammel
The old twat of a camel,
And then she could screw the whole city.

Nell

There was a young lady named Nell
Whose panties were holey as hell.
She complained, "When I fart,
My shoes fall apart,
And my ankles occasionally swell."

Nero

Consider the Emperor Nero
(Of many lewd tales he's the hero);
Though he scraped the fiddle,
He just couldn't diddle,
And his real batting average was zero.

ne's'ry

Said a jealous old maid, "Men aren't ne's'ry,
And a penis is just an accessory.
For freedom from fear
And a thrill in the rear,
I'll stick to my old rubber pessary."

neuter

A young man who feared he was neuter
Fed his vital facts to a computer.
The machine, like a flash,
Typed, "Forget about gash . . .
You'll be Fag-of-the-Year as a fruiter."

Nice

A fisherman in medieval Nice
Was instantly ordered to cease
His naughty deception
When, during inspection,
They found a real cod in his piece.

niece

Have you heard of Tolstoi's lovely niece,
A delectable morsel named Lys?
Need I say more?
She was the war,
And Tolstoi was the one got the peace.

Norway

There was a young lady of Norway
Who hung by her heels in a doorway.
She said to her beau,
"Just look at me, Joe.
I think I've discovered one more way."

Notre Dame

Abailardus of old Notre Dame
Was proud of his scholarly fame,
'Til he got him a piece
From the canon's sweet niece,
And lost both his stones for the same.

Oak

A speedy young jeweler named Oak
Fixed clocks that were damaged and broke.
He opened the face
And in a short space
He changed hands without missing a stroke.

obscene

Old King Louis and court were obscene;
They would screw day and night . . .
and the queen!
But they made one great error;
They hung round for the Terror—
Guillotine! Guillotine! Guillotine!

Oedipus Rex

The play about Oedipus Rex
Has a plot that is very complex.
He clobbered his pa,
And then screwed his ma,
While the Chorus sang songs about sex.

offer

Some writers have romance to offer;
Black humor is all I can proffer.
Let's all laugh at the Snopes,
Those hilarious dopes
From Yok-Yok-Yok-Yoknapatawpha.

Oklahoma

A lady from West Oklahoma
Always came when she heard "La Paloma."
Once, in Mexico City—
Ah! More is the pity—
The lady stayed in a deep coma.

O'Quim

Shed a tear for Teresa O'Quim
Who jumped from a boat for a swim,
Got herself in a jam
With her hand in a clam,
Now seaweed grows out of her quim.

Ostend

There was a young girl of Ostend
Who her maidenhead tried to defend,
But a chasseur d'Afrique
Inserted his prique
And taught that ex-maid how to spend.

Ostend

There was a young man of Ostend
Whose wife caught him fucking her friend.
"It's no use, my duck,
Interrupting our fuck,
For I'm damned if I draw 'til I spend."

parentis

Said two farm boys, *in loco parentis,*
"These new words are gonna dement us—
Like ordure and offal;
They sound just plain awful.
It is driving us *non compost mentis.*"

Parma

There was a young warrior of Parma
Who got into bed with his charmer.
She—naturally—nude,
Said, "Don't think me rude,
But I *do* wish you'd take off your armor."

Parmimahanda

A yogi named Parmimahanda
Thought love with a cobra was danda,
'Til a flick of the fang
In the shank of the yang
Left him dead upon the veranda.

Pease

A zoology major named Pease
Begged her prof for a couple of B's.
He toyed with her C,
Then showed her his D;
She was finally bedded with E's.

Peck

There was a young sailor named Peck
Who kept his passions in check
By thinking of rumors
Of penile tumors,
And beating his meat below deck.

Penzance

There was a young girl of Penzance
Who boarded a bus in a trance.
The passengers fucked her,
Likewise the conductor;
The driver shot off in his pants.

Penzance

There was a young man of Penzance
Who rogered his three maiden aunts.
Though them he defiled,
He ne'er got them with child,
Through using the letters of France.

Persians

A remarkable race are the Persians;
They have such peculiar diversions.
They screw the whole day
In the regular way,
And save up the nights for perversions.

Peru

A rabbi who lived in Peru
Was vainly attempting to screw.
His wife said, "Oy veh!
If you keep on this way,
The Messiah will come before you."

Peru

Said a classicist down in Peru,
"When in love you can best follow through
And show your devotion
With the helical motion
Of the great Archimedean screw."

Peru

There was a young girl from Peru
Who regretted her lovers were few,
So she walked from her door,
With a fig leaf, no more,
And now she's in bed . . . with the flu.

Peru

There was a young man of Peru
Who was hard up for something to do,
So he took out his carrot
And buggered his parrot,
And sent the results to the zoo.

pet

The Venusians do not kiss or pet
Or work themselves up in a sweat
About sex; they get wed,
Then all feeling goes dead;
How alien, heck! can you get?

Pete

There was a young fellow named Pete
Who took a flashlight 'neath the sheet.
When asked to tell why,
This was his reply,
"I'm all right if I watch what I eat."

Phidias

There once was a sculptor named Phidias,
Whose knowledge of art was invidious.
On a statue of Venus
He carved a huge penis,
Thus shocking the ultra-fastidious.

Phipps

At death's door lay Alicia Phipps.
No man had yet mounted her hips.
As sadly she waited,
One intern palpitated;
She died with a smile on her lips.

picture palaces

The girls who frequent picture palaces
Set no store by psychoanalysis,
And though Mr. Freud
Is greatly annoyed,
They cling to their old-fashioned phalluses.

Pisces

A lesbian born under Pisces
Has dildoes of several sizes.
The one with the warts
Squirts several quarts,
And gives all her girl friends surprises.

plainer

"Each year," said a Wells girl, "it's plainer;
Cramming's vain, class attendance is vainer.
To get A in Phys Ed
I just worked out in bed
With the wrestling coach and the trainer."

plastered

The bachelor girl who gets plastered
And fears she'll be screwed by some bastard
Should get her physician
To make an incision,
And be doctored before she is mastered.

Poitan

The College of Arms of Poitan
Ennobled a lowly-born man
Because (we are told)
He handed out gold
And slave girls who danced with a fan.

Polyp

An irate young husband named Polyp
Lashed out with a terrible wallop
At an overnight guest
Who dared to suggest
That his wife was an *ord'nary* trollop.

Poole

An English conductor named Poole
Conducted Brahms's *First* with his tool.
Such ambidexterity,
Grace, and celerity!
(The critical comment was cool.)

popsicles

A divorcée, as cold as popsicles,
Waived all her ex-husband's nickels.
She transplanted, instead,
To each side of her head,
Two earrings carved from his testicles.

Port Said

There was a young man of Port Said
Whose penis grew tattered and frayed,
Thus earning him taunts
From his well-meaning aunts,
And complaints from the women he laid.

Pratt

A sharp old musician named Pratt
Had a staff that was breve but fat.
Though he owned a château,
He felt obbligato
To bugger his boy in A-flat.

pretty

She wasn't what one would call pretty,
And other girls offered her pity,
So nobody guessed
That her Wassermann test
Involved half of the men in the city.

Proctor

A patient of young Doctor Proctor
Didn't mind when he swiftly unfroctor.
Nor did his technique
Give her reason to squique,
Until *after* she found he'd upknocktor.

proportions

Cecilia of ample proportions
Took all contraceptive precautions,
But thin little Ermintrude
Let a small sperm intrude.
Do you know a good man for abortions?

Purdue

Said a passionate girl from Purdue
To her German professor, Karl Drew,
"You think reading Nietzsche
Is perfectly peachy,
But, frankly, I'd much rather screw."

Purdue

There was a young man from Purdue,
Who was only just learning to screw,
But he hadn't the knack;
He got too far back . . .
The right church, so to speak, but wrong pew.

Racine

There was a young man from Racine
Who invented a fucking machine.
Concave or convex,
It would fit either sex,
And was perfectly simple to clean.

Racine

There was a young man of Racine
Who was weaned at the age of sixteen.
He said, "I'll admit
There's no milk in the tit,
But think of the fun it has been!"

Raines

An ardent campaigner named Raines,
When parading for feminine gains,
Was arrested at once
For engaging in stunts
That left several permanent stains.

Raleigh

A well-bred young miss from old Raleigh
Met a man from New York on the traleigh.
When she said to the guy,
"Y'all come, don't be shy,"
He gave her a valeigh, by galeigh!

Rangoon

There was a young man from Rangoon,
Whose farts could be heard to the moon.
When you wouldn't expect 'em,
They would rush from his rectum,
Like the roar of a double bassoon.

Ransom

There was a young lady named Ransom,
Who was rogered three times in a hansom.
When she cried out for more,
A voice from the floor
Said, "My name is Simpson . . . not Samson."

ranted

A well-known mesmerist ranted
That a spell could not be recanted.
"Could it be?" was the question,
"Post-hypnotic suggestion
Is a thought that's forever trance-planted?"

Rape

The duchess of Whiteside cried, "Rape!"
When she found in her bedroom an ape.
The ape said, "You ass!
Go look in the glass,"
And left by the fire escape.

Rawls

There was a young fellow named Rawls,
Who slipped from the dome of St. Paul's,
But the angels of grace
Sped thither apace,
And lowered him down by the balls.

Reading

There was a young fellow of Reading
Who grew so aroused at his wedding;
At the sight of his bride,
When he got her inside,
He creamed all over the bedding.

Reilly

There once was a widow named Reilly,
Who esteemed her late husband most highly,
And, in spite of the scandal,
Her umbrella handle
Was made of his *membrum virile.*

remembers

Said an old maid one fondly remembers,
"Now my days are quite clearly Septembers.
All my fires have burned low,
I'll admit that it's so,
But you still might have fun in the embers."

renown

There was a young girl of renown
Who'd been had by most men in town.
Her morals were loose
As the bowels of a goose,
And her eyes were a sad rectum-brown.

Rex

A young Scottish soldier named Rex
Abstains with great zeal from all sex.
He is such a Spartan
Because of his tartan;
He suffers from a kilt complex.

Rheims

A crafty old bugler of Rheims
Would feast upon coconut creams,
And fart a toccata
Or a Mozart sonata
On seventeenth-century themes.

Rheims

There was a young fellow of Rheims
Who was terribly plagued with wet dreams.
He saved up a dozen
And sent to his cousin,
Who ate them and thought they were creams.

Rhyll

There was a young lady of Rhyll,
In an omnibus was taken ill,
So she called the conductor,
Who got in and fucked her,
Which did her more good than a pill.

Rio

A young violinist from Rio
Was seducing a lady named Cleo.
As she took down her panties,
She said, "No *andantes;*
I want this *allegro con brio.*"

Ritz

There was a young man from the Ritz
Who planted an acre of tits.
They came up in the fall,
Red nipples and all,
And he leisurely chewed them to bits.

Robin Hood

A bandit was bold Robin Hood,
Whose motives were misunderstood.
He took tons of riches
From rich sons-of-bitches,
And reviled them while pulling his pud.

Rodgers

There once was a young girl named Rodgers,
An apprentice who played with the lodgers,
And two who were able
Slipped under the table,
To the horror of several old codgers.

rolled rug

I breathe as though wrapped in a rolled rug;
My nose is stopped up like an old jug.
I must stop my ravin';
It's dreamland I'm cravin'
But how can I sleep with this cold bug?

Roos

A miscegenator named Roos
Spent a week in Rangoon on the loose
After trying all races
On an impartial basis,
His favorite hue remains puce.

Rowell

A certain young lady named Rowell
Had a musical vent to her bowel.
With a good plate of beans
Tucked under her jeans,
She could play "To a Wild Rose" by
MacDowell.

rumming

Are you looking for wenching and rumming?
In Ind, you'll find everything humming.
With a Hindu gal, sex
Is so gaily complex,
You won't know if you're going or coming.

Russell

To probe Miss Lillian Russell,
Dr. Long thrust a pin through her bustle.
He got a sprained wrist,
And a mouthful of fist,
For the bustle turned out to be muscle.

Sagittarius

The men of the sign Sagittarius
Have customs obscene and barbarious.
They sow their wild oats
With girls, boys, and goats,
In postures ingenious and various.

St. Bees

There was an old man of St. Bees,
Who was stung in the arm by a wasp.
When asked, "Does it hurt?"
He replied, "No, it doesn't.
I'm so glad it wasn't a hornet."

St. Bees

There was a young *man* of St. Bees,
Who said to his girl, "If you please,
While playing with this,
It would give me great bliss,
If you'd pay some attention to these."

There was a young *girl* of St. Bees,
Who said to her beau, "If you please,
While playing with this,
It would give me great bliss,
If you'd pay some attention to these."

St. John's

There was a young lad of St. John's
Who wanted to bugger the swans,
But the loyal hall porter
Said, "No! Take my daughter.
Them birds is reserved for the dons."

St. Paul

An original miss from St. Paul
Wore a newspaper dress to a ball,
But the dress caught on fire,
And burnt her entire,
Front page, sports section, and all.

St. Paul

There was an old maid from St. Paul
Who went to the birth-control ball.
She was loaded with pessaries
And other accessories,
But nobody asked her at all.

St. Paul

There was a young man from St. Paul
Who went to a fancy dress ball.
He went off in his pants
In the midst of a dance,
And had to go home in a shawl.

St. Paul's

Said the venerable dean of St. Paul's,
"Concerning them cracks in the walls,
Do you think it would do
If we filled them with glue?"
The bishop of London said, "Balls."

St. Paul's

There was a young man of St. Paul's,
Who dreamt of Niagara Falls.
When he woke the next day,
It was "Anchors Aweigh"
For his penis, his ass, and his balls.

Saki

In a scene reminiscent of Saki,
Malformed Joe saw Doctor de Bakey,
Then used his transplant
To deflower his aunt,
And took off for Paris, quite cocky.

sallow

A bull-dyke of complexion sallow
Screamed, "Pricks are like wicks without tallow.
Why, all men admit
They'd prefer a clit."
(That's something I find hard to swallow.)

Sally

There was a young matron named Sally,
Who went with her groom up an alley.
There was naught she could do;
He was too young to screw.
She muttered, "How Green Was My Valet."

Samoa

There was a young girl of Samoa
Who boasted that no man could know her.
One young fellow tried,
But she wriggled aside,
And spilled all his spermatozoa.

Sans Souci

Said a Frenchman who lived at Sans Souci,
"Superstition? Mon Dieu! C'est tout fou, si?
Why only ce soir
I buggaired un chat noir;
To un homme virile, poussy is poussy."

scarred

A northerner, ragged and scarred,
Displayed to a wandering bard
A shield for his back,
All battered and black,
And remarked it was called his Asgard.

Schiff

An arrogant Nazi named Schiff
Broke up with his wife in a tiff.
Though he did not lack charm,
She complained that his arm
Was the only thing he could keep stiff.

Scot

There once was a wily old Scot,
Who took a young girl on his yacht.
Too lazy to rape her,
He made darts out of paper,
Which he languidly tossed at her twat.

screw

He was known as a wonderful screw,
With his dink in the pink all day through,
But the fine days of plenty
Were done after twenty,
When the red in his balls turned to blue.

screw

The right to decide when to screw
Is one that the femmes now pursue.
If the girls get the voice
In making that choice,
It won't be how much, but with who.

sea

There was a young lady at sea,
Who complained that it hurt her to pee.
"Aha!" said the mate,
"*That* accounts for the state
Of the captain, the boatswain, and me."

Sears

In the catalogue published by Sears,
A layout by Dali appears.
It depicts a June bride
With three breasts on each side,
Caressing a penis with ears.

Seattle

There was a young man from Seattle,
Whose balls were so small they would rattle
He tried 'em on chickens,
Got good as the dickens,
And now he can satisfy cattle.

seem

Oh, Shakespeare's love life, it would seem,
Was something not quite on the beam.
Too lazy to fuck,
And not wanting to suck,
He preferred *A Midsummer Night's Dream.*

serene

Said Napoleon, emperor serene,
While scouting around for a queen,
"I'd much rather squeeza
Maria Louisa,
Than sleep with that bitch Josephine."

Set

There once was a priestess of Set
Whom a shaman pursued on a bet.
Though she turned to a snake,
The shaman won the stake,
But it's something he'd rather forget.

Shafter

Tim said to his wife, up in Shafter,
"Seems to me there's a man in the rafter."
She smirked, and then said,
"Come, get into bed;
I'm saving that fellow for after."

Shalott

There was a young maid from Shalott,
Who claimed she was hotter than hot.
She burnt off the hair
Of a priest from Adair,
Who said it was worth what he got . . .
She burnt off the balls
Of a priest from St. Paul's,
Who mournfully said it was not.

Shaw

Cried a great English writer, "Oh, Shaw!
My testes are small as the Dickens."
Said his surgeon, "Great Scott!
Here's a fine pair-o'-Keats';
I'll transplant them and make your Balsworthy."

Sheba

There was a young woman named Sheba
Who loved a Teutonic amoeba.
This primordial jelly
Would crawl on her belly,
And murmur, "Ich liebe, ich liebe."

shrew

The tiniest animal, the shrew,
Is known for the three-second screw.
He'll repeat it at will,
On any mole hill,
And his head is all that turns blue.

Siam

There was a young maiden from Siam,
Who said to her lover, young Khayyam,
"To seduce me, of course,
You will have to use force.
Thank goodness you're stronger than I am."

Siam

These words spoke the king of Siam,
"For women I don't care a damn,
But a fat-bottomed boy
Is my pride and my joy.
You may call me a bugger. I am!"

Siberia

There was a young monk of Siberia,
Whose life grew drearier and drearier,
So he did to a nun
What he shouldn't have done,
And made her a Mother Superior.

Sidney

There was an old fellow named Sidney,
Who drank 'til he ruined a kidney.
It shriveled and shrank
As he sat there and drank,
But he had a good time of it, didn't he?

sin

To the doc said his wife, "It's a sin,
But I don't want a baby again.
To help save our marriage,
Take my baby carriage,
But I still want to keep my play pen."

Sioux

An Indian maiden, a Sioux,
As tempting as fresh honeydioux,
Liked to show off her knees,
As she strolled past tepees,
And hear the braves holler, "Wioux, Wioux!"

Sioux

There once was a sensuous Sioux
Who liked to do nothing but scrioux;
She would give no relief
To her favorite chief,
Until both of his balls had turned blioux.

site

(From a Tourist Guide Book)

"This theater is a state landmark site."
"The box office is just to your right."
"The first show is at ten."
"Where's the room of the men?"
"Do you have any seats for tonight?"

Skinner

There was a young fellow named Skinner
Who took a young lady to dinner.
They sat down to dine
At a quarter past nine,
At a quarter past ten it was in her (the dinner,
not Skinner),
Skinner was in her before dinner.

(As retold)
There was a young fellow named Tupper
Who took a young lady to supper.
They sat down to dine
At a quarter past nine,
At a quarter to ten, it was up her; not the supper,
not Tupper,
But some son-of-a-bitch named Skinner.

Slough

There was a young lady of Slough,
Who said that she didn't know how.
Then a young fellow caught her,
And jolly well taught her;
She lodges in Pimlico now.

small

The Plutonian male is so small
He lives in the vaginal wall
Of his mate. Yes, *de trop,*
But he *likes* it, you know,
And *chacun à son goût,* after all.

Smith

At Wellesley, Vassar, and Smith,
A common and recurring myth
That a masculine member
Helps students remember
Was found without substance or pith.

Smith

Said a pretty young student from Smith,
Whose virtue was largely a myth,
"Try hard as I can,
I can't find a man
Whom it's fun to be virtuous with."

some

A cabby's wife, brighter than some,
Had a meter installed in her bum,
With a musical chime
To keep track of the time
And allow you to pay as you come.

Sondant

A tragic young wife, Mrs. Sondant,
Made complaint in an accent despondent.
The courtroom was sultry;
The charge was adultery—
Her brother was named co-respondent.

Soo

A heifer from up near the Soo,
When approached by a bull, answered, "Moo."
Then she took the wrong tack,
And lay down on her back . . .
But the bull figured out what to do.

soul

Confession is good for the soul.
I admit that I've dreamed of a hole
That was not round but square,
And had silky green hair
So thick it was like a mink stole.

Souling

Said an eager young surgeon from Souling,
"So far, we have only been fooling.
Soon it won't vex us
To change both the sexes,
It's simply a case of retooling."

South Dakota

A coed from U. South Dakota
Collected a clutch of male scrota.
The hairy old hide
She opened and dried
And the contents she used for pelota.

South Forks

There's a woman who lives at South Forks
Makes a fetish of old vermouth corks.
She keeps those labeled *France*
In the front of her pants,
And *Italy* back round her porks.

South Joisey

A railroad hotel in South Joisey
's near where they switch trains and is noisy.
A guest phoned the clerk
And yelled, "Hey, you jerk!
When's this damn hotel get to Boise?"

Spain

Then up spoke the young king of Spain,
"To fuck and to bugger is pain.
But it's not *infra dig*
On occasion to frig,
And I do it again and again."

Spain

There was a young lady of Spain
Who took down her pants on a train.
A very young porter
Saw more than he orter,
And asked her to do it again.

Spain

There was a young lady from Spain
Who did it again and again.
And again and again
And again and again
And again and again and again.

spectra

With color enough for twin spectra,
This plane really needs nothing extra.
As I walk to the back,
I rejoice I wore black,
For my mourning becomes Electra.

Spitzbergen

There was a young girl of Spitzbergen
Whose people all thought her a virgin,
'Til they found her in bed
With her quim very red
And the head of a kid just emergin'.

star

As a beauty, I am not a star;
There are others more handsome by far.
But my face, I don't mind it,
You see, I'm behind it;
It's the fellow in front gets the jar.

state

"Miss Smith," said the dean, "I must state
As a scholar you don't pull much weight.
Your math is just terrible,
Your physics unbearable,
Though I'd say your physique is just great."

stating

A problem that's very worth stating,
Researching, exploring, debating,
Is if we can tell,
From our friends with one cell,
Whether splitting's as much fun as mating.

Stead

For a phallus, Miss Winifred Stead
Used a bar from the foot of her bed,
But lacking the touch
Of blacksmiths and such
Kept her ever from forging ahead.

stifled

At last, when his moaning was stifled,
He groaned, "I would never have trifled
With Hortense the whore,
And gotten so sore,
If I'd known her vagina was rifled."

Stone

Said a haughty old lecher named Stone,
Who had but five inches of bone,
"I feel no deep urgin'
To consult a surgeon;
A mighty poor thing, but mine own!"

stop

Junior's sex in my auto must stop
Or my son must locate a new prop.
It is a convertible,
And what's disconcertible
Are the high-heel holes thrust through the top.

strange

The formula's secret and strange,
It's cooked on an old-fashioned range,
And makes use of juices
That come from abuses,
Plus hair from a dog with the mange.

Strensall

There was a young fellow of Strensall
Whose prick was as sharp as a pencil.
On the night of his wedding,
It went through the bedding
And shattered the bedroom utensil.

strewed

A bather whose clothing was strewed
By breezes that left her quite nude
Saw a man come along
And, unless I am wrong,
You expected this line to be lewd.

Stroud

There was a young fellow from Stroud,
Who was feeling his girl in a crowd.
A fellow up front
Said, "Hmmmm . . . Smell a cunt."
Just like that; very soft; not loud.

Stutz

A Women's Lib leader named Stutz
Is known to have plenty of guts.
When asked what she'd need
To be totally freed,
She snarls at her questioner, "Nuts!"

Stylites

On his pillar sat Simon Stylites,
As his balls turned to iron pyrites,
And the sun's intense heat
Slowly blackened his meat;
He should not have worn French lace nighties.

sublime

A whore had the notion sublime
To take seven men at one time;
One on top, one beneath,
In each hand, in the teeth,
And two with her toes, for a dime.

surprised

A friend of ours once was surprised
To have his long dong criticized
By a whore who was shrewish,
Too fat, and half Jewish,
Because it was uncircumcised.

Suzie

The police arrested young Suzie
For being a militant floozie.
They took off her clothes,
But no record shows
There was fuzz on top of her coozie.

Sweet Briar

"We are ladies here at Sweet Briar,"
The dean told the girls. "We require
That you peddle your ass,
If you must, outside class,
And, at all times, in formal attire."

Swoboda

There was an old man of Swoboda,
Who'd not pay a whore what he owed her,
So, with great savoir faire,
She climbed up on a chair,
And pissed in his whisky and soda.

Sydney

There was a young lady from Sydney,
Who had it rammed up to her kidney.
Then a man from Quebec
Rammed it up to her neck.
My! *He* had a long one, didn't he?

Tarsus

There was a young fellow of Tarsus,
Who felt that he needed catharsis.
To achieve the purge royal,
He took croton oil,
Discovering, too late, 'twas for horses.

tart

Though a biblical strip-teasing tart,
Salome was a girl with great heart.
The truth is that instead
Of John the Baptist's head,
She had asked a more pertinent part.

taste

There was a young lady of taste,
Who kept herself virgin and chaste,
And stoutly defended
With bear-traps suspended
By filigree chains from her waist.

Taurus

A man of the natal sign Taurus
Joined up with a folk singing chorus,
But he didn't last long,
For in every song
He croaked like an old brontosaurus.

tea

We invited the duchess to tea.
It was just as I feared it would be;
Her rumblings abdominal
Were simply abominable,
And everyone thought it was me.

Ted

Said a just-wed professor named Ted,
To a redhead coed in his bed,
"The weather's so snowy,
And gusty and blowy,
Won't you swallow my pride, dear, instead?"

teens

Our most existentialist teens
Are impatient of lectures by deans
On restraining desires
And banking the fires
That burn in their skirts and their jeans.

So they go on exerting their wills
And they use neither condoms nor pills.
The results are most dire;
They become dam and sire,
And their parents just pick up the bills.

Thalia

There was a Greek sailor from Thalia
Who had several ways to regale ya.
The best thing about him
Was a dainty small quim
Just above his huge male genitalia.

Tharp

A lady musician named Tharp
Got her bust tangled up in her harp.
Though protest arose,
She was forced to transpose
Bach's G-Minor Suite to C-sharp.

three

On Saturn the sexes are three,
A sad state of affairs, you'll agree.
For performing *con brio,*
You must have a trio,
And it even takes two for a pee.

Thun

There was a young lady of Thun
Who was blocked by the man in the moon.
"Well, it has been great fun,"
She remarked when he'd done,
"But I'm sorry you came quite so soon."

Tibet

There was a young man of Tibet—
And this is the strangest one yet—
His prick was so long,
And so pointed and strong,
He could bugger six Greeks *en brochette.*

Tipple

A Northampton professor named Tipple
Loved to suckle a student's left nipple.
Though he did it with ardor,
He could not get it harder,
And he came without even a ripple.

tit

My girl friend's astonishing tit
Was as tough as an old catcher's mitt;
The other was lighter
And softer and whiter.
I wonder what happened to it?

Tottenham

There was a young person of Tottenham
Whose manners, Good Lord! she'd forgotten 'em.
When she went to the vicar's,
She took off her knickers,
Because, she said, she was hot in 'em.

toucan

A marvelous bird is the toucan
Who when engaged in a screw can
Stand upon his head,
Shove beak in instead;
If you think that's a cinch, see if you can.

trafficker

In limericks I'm not a trafficker
For my nature is really seraphicker.
My stomach sits queasily,
I blush far too easily,
And I do not collect pornographicker.

Tralee

There was a young girl of Tralee,
Whose knowledge of French was "Oui, oui."
When they asked, "Parlez-vous?"
She replied, "Same to you,"
And was famed for her bright repartee.

transplants

In these days of grafts and transplants,
A guy really takes quite a chance.
Are the charms of his toots
The original goods,
Or are they from one of his aunts?

Trask

Said an ardent bridegroom named Trask,
"I will grant any boon that you ask."
Said his bride, "Fuck me, dearie,
Until I grow weary."
He died of old age at the task.

Tring

There was a young lady of Tring
Who sat by the fire to sing.
A piece of charcoal
Flew right up her hole,
And burnt all the hair off her quim.

Troy

There was a young lady of Troy,
Who invented a new kind of joy.
She sugared her quim,
Both outside and in,
And then had it sucked by a boy.

try

The Church, after many a try,
Has developed a birth-control buy
That's in no way mechanical,
Though goddamned satanical;
On the end of the dong, graft an eye.

Tucker

There was an inventor named Tucker
Who built a vagina of yucca,
But his words were obscene
When the fractious machine
Got a grip and refused to unpucker.

Tuphet

There was a young lady from Tuphet,
Whose box was so huge none could stuff it.
They transplanted the twidget
Of a rather small midget.
Now she's known as Little Miss Muffit.

Tupps

A broken-down harlot named Tupps
Was heard to confess, in her cups,
"The height of my folly
Was screwing a collie,
But I got a good price for the pups."

tutor

A fine young university tutor
Fed his sex history to a computer.
Due to pulse-circuit stalls,
It reprogrammed his balls,
And he found himself totally neuter.

Twickenham

There was a young lady of Twickenham,
Who regretted that men had no prick in 'em.
On her knees, every day
To God she would pray
To lengthen and strengthen and thicken 'em.

Two Cities

The title *A Tale of Two Cities*
Tends to fill me with numerous pities.
If I had the pickins
(Instead of Charles Dickens),
I'd call it *One Tail and Two Titties.*

Tyson

There was a young harlot named Tyson
Who conceived mad love for a bison.
After love's fruition,
Her snatch's condition
Was never again so enticing.

unclose

The pink buds have refused to unclose,
The aroma's not much of a *chose.*
Gardening's been luckless
For Alice B. Toklas,
Still, a rose is a rose is a rose.

Ur

There was a young fellow of Ur
Whose Charley was covered with fur.
He delighted to stroke it,
To pat and to poke it,
For the pleasure of hearing it purr.

Vassar

A misanthrope teaching at Vassar
Was implored by a nymph to please pass her.
The ill-tempered old grouch
Threw her down on a couch
And bounced on her antimacassar.

Venus

There was a young spaceman from Venus
Who had a prodigious penis.
Cried his girl friend, "Alas!
It just came out my ass,
And there's still fifteen inches between us."

Verdun

A skinny old maid from Verdun
Wed a short-peckered son-of-a-gun.
She said, "I don't care
If there isn't much there;
God knows, it is better than none."

Versailles

A pretty girl touring Versailles
Remarked, "It's too bad; I could cry.
I've been here ten days
And not gone to the Louvre."
"Never mind," somebody said, "it's probably
only the hard water."

viable

Since transplanting has proved to be viable,
And my dong's been less plied than pliable,
Why not graft, as a ringer,
My trusty third finger,
Which, these days, is far more reliable?

vicious

Said the Skidmore prof, "I'm not vicious,
But short skirts bring visions lubricious.
When I look down my class
At those acres of ass,
I come in my pants. It's delicious."

vote

My Grandmother fought for the vote,
Then my Mother bought gin off the boat.
Today, my dear Wife
Says I've ruined her life,
And my Daughter's applying to Choate.

Vundrum

A famous zoologist, Vundrum,
Was posed a perplexing conundrum:
Where to locate what falls
From an elephant's balls.
And he said, "Vy, it's zimple; look undrum."

wall

(Mene mene tekel upharsin)

Read the message that's writ on the wall,
In fiery script ten feet tall,
And, in case Hebrew
Is all Greek to you,
I'll translate: It says *Fuck You All.*

Walt

A Civil War nurse, by name Walt,
Said, "It really isn't my fault.
In wartime, it is clear,
Those we stick in the rear
Are the sick, and the lame, and the halt."

waters

Come to Noah's for wine and strong waters,
And for diddling in clean, classy quarters.
I assure every guest
I've made personal test
Of my booze, and my beds, and my daughters.

way

To be your own man is the way
To feel like a king every day.
Don't be your own queen,
Not that it's unclean,
But a girl's got a right to a lay.

Weem

A dashing young fellow named Weem
Every night had a luscious wet dream.
'Til a friend, quite annoyed,
Hired a disciple of Freud,
Who cured him, which I think is mean.

weird

Now wouldn't a lady look weird
If she grew a mustache and a beard?
Yet, if some of the militants
Lost all their depilatants,
I think their whole game would be queered.

Wells

The bishop of Bath and of Wells
Used to suffer from frenetic spells,
And the only quick cure
Of which he was sure
Was to fondle his monks in their cells.

West

There was an old critic named West
Whose penis came up to his chest.
He said, "I declare,
I have no pubic hair,"
So he covered his nuts with his vest.

whale

Jonah mused, as he cruised through the whale,
"I'm in guts to my nuts in this jail,
But I'll pass through the ass
In a mass of hot gas,
And depart with a fart through the tail."

White

An oversexed lady named White
Insists on a dozen a night.
A fellow named Cheddar
Had the brashness to wed her;
His chance of survival is slight.

whore

An insatiable Elsinore whore
Once toured with the Met's *Trovatore,*
But when she got through
With a tenor she knew,
She thought she had done *Le Coq d'Or.*

Wilde

Said an unwed campaigner named Wilde,
"I'm not upset at being defiled.
They'll find a solution
To every pollution,
Until then, what to do with the child?"

Wilde

There was a young lady named Wilde
Who kept herself quite undefiled
By thinking of Jesus,
Contagious diseases,
And the bother of having a child.

willow

While Mabel lay prone 'neath a willow,
She was screwed by a large armadillo,
And remarked to the same,
As the two of them came,
That the next time he might bring a pillow.

Wimley

A wanton young lady from Wimley,
Reproached for not acting quite primly,
Answered, "Heavens above,
I know sex isn't love,
But it's such an attractive facsimile."

win

Now at college a girl just can't win,
What with studies and sex and bad gin.
And it's just the last straw
When the dean says, "Withdraw!"
When it's him that's been sticking it in.

wise

There was a young tutor, most wise,
Who loved to feel cocks, just for size.
At every school dance,
He'd unzip the boys' pants;
They nicknamed him *Lord of the Flies*.

Wokingham

There is a new baron of Wokingham;
The girls say he don't care for poking 'em,
Preferring "Minette,"*
Which is pleasant, but yet,
There is one disadvantage—choking 'em.

*Equivalent to fellatio

Worcester

There was a young lady of Worcester,
Who dreamt that a rooster sedorcester.
She awoke with a scream,
But 'twas only a dream;
A bump in the mattress had gorcester.

Wynn

Full ninety years old was friend Wynn
When he went to a hookshop to sin.
But, try as he would,
It did him no good,
For all he had left was the skin.

Yale

There was a professor from Yale
Who searched for a fresh piece of tail.
He found in his class
A young piece of ass;
Now he's spending his spare time in jail.

Yale

There was a young fellow from Yale
Whose face was exceedingly pale.
He spent his vacation
In self-masturbation,
Because of the high price of tail.

years

While musicians have battled for years
Over which are the best symphoneers,
They agree from the start
That a "Whistling Fart"
Is great music to all of their rears.

yelling

For sex our man Joe's always yelling.
At the sight of the breast's slightest swelling,
He would pull out his cock
From the top of his sock,
Then what he would do, there's no telling.

York

There was a young lady of York
Who plugged herself up with a cork.
She explained, "It's more svelte
Than a chastity belt,
And is quickly removed with a fork."

youth

An exuberant Westminster youth
Laid his girl in a telephone booth.
When he pressed button "B,"
She reacted with glee,
Though onlookers termed it uncouth.

Yuma

There was a young fellow from Yuma,
Who essayed to bugger a puma.
In the midst of the frolics,
It clawed off his bollics;
An example of animal humor.

PERSONAL LIMERICKS

LIMERICKS TO BE COMPLETED

A horny young stud, name of Bower,
Had his tool fall off in the shower.
The replacement was thin.
Said his doc, "What a sin

___

ADDITIONAL LINES

___

*(Name)*___

___

*(Name)*___

___

*(Name)*___

___

*(Name)*___

___

*(Name)*___

There was a young man from the docks
Who could not get into a box.
Said he, "For a nickel,
I'd take an old pickle

____

ADDITIONAL LINES

____

*(Name)*______________________________

____

*(Name)*______________________________

____

*(Name)*______________________________

____

*(Name)*______________________________

____

*(Name)*______________________________

____

*(Name)*______________________________

A poet, by birthright a Scorpio,
Was trying to rhyme the word "Scorpio."
He tried and he tried
'Til, in torment, he died,

____

ADDITIONAL LINES

____

*(Name)*______________________

____

*(Name)*______________________

____

*(Name)*______________________

____

*(Name)*______________________

____

*(Name)*______________________

____

*(Name)*______________________

There was a young fop from Kildare,
Who never stopped combing his hair.
Then he put on a wig,
And remarked to his pig,

____

ADDITIONAL LINES

____

*(Name)*______________________________

____

*(Name)*______________________________

____

*(Name)*______________________________

____

*(Name)*______________________________

____

*(Name)*______________________________

____

*(Name)*______________________________

Said the pope to a banker in Rome,
"St. Pete's needs a new gilded dome,
The Swiss guards are bitter,
I need a new litter,

____

ADDITIONAL LINES

____

*(Name)*______________________________

____

*(Name)*______________________________

____

*(Name)*______________________________

____

*(Name)*______________________________

____

*(Name)*______________________________

____

*(Name)*______________________________

There was a young man from Fall River,
Whose tool was as thin as a sliver.
It would dart in and out
Like a speckled brook trout,

____

ADDITIONAL LINES

____

*(Name)*______________________________

____

*(Name)*______________________________

____

*(Name)*______________________________

____

*(Name)*______________________________

____

*(Name)*______________________________

____

*(Name)*______________________________

An Amazon living in Chad,
Was wooed by a primitive lad:
She said, "Tho' you dig me,
My God! You're a pygmy."

ADDITIONAL LINES

---

*(Name)*__________

---

*(Name)*__________

---

*(Name)*__________

---

*(Name)*__________

---

*(Name)*__________

---

*(Name)*__________

A SELECTED BIBLIOGRAPHY

Aiken, Conrad.
A Seizure of Limericks.
New York: Holt, Rinehart & Winston, 1964.

Anonymous.
To Solace the Blind.
Frankfurt-am-Main, 1945.

Baring-Gould, W. S.
The Lure of the Limerick.
New York: Clarkson N. Potter, 1967.

Cerf, Bennett.
Out on a Limerick.
New York: Harper & Row, 1960.

Douglas, Norman.
Some Limericks.
Paris: Le Ballet des Muses, 1964.

Holland, Vyvyan.
An Explosion of Limerick.
New York: Funk & Wagnalls, 1967.

Legman, Gershon.
The Limerick.
Paris: Les Hautes Etudes, 1953; New York: Brandywine Press, 41 West 58th Street, New York, N.Y. 10019.

The Pearl:
A Journal of Voluptuous Reading.
New York: Grove Press, 1968.

Vicarion, Count Palmira.
Book of Limericks.
Paris: The Olympia Press, 1956.

Wells, Carolyn.
Book of American Limericks.
New York: G. P. Putnam's Sons, 1925.

ROLL OF HONOR

In addition to those eminent scholars, cited in the Bibliography, who have edited books of limericks—often enriching them with their own compositions—the following composers of limericks, many of whom are represented in this volume, deserve highest recognition and acclaim:

Aldiss, Brian W.
Anderson, Mary
Anderson, Poul
Anon.
Armstrong, Robert Plant
Auden, W. H.
Benson, Doug
Billington, Raymond A.
Bishop, Morris
Boardman, George
Burgess, Gelett
Carter, Harvey L.
Daniels, R. Balfour
Davies, Randall
Dressler, David
Fadiman, Clifton
Field, Eugene
Gilbert and Sullivan
Gorey, Edward
Herford, Oliver
Kimpton, Lawrence
Knox, Ronald
Lear, Edward
Lehrman, Nat
Linden, Rick
Members of the Society of the Fifth Line
Nash, Ogden
Reed, H. Langford
Seabury, Paul
Shaw, George Bernard
Spectorsky, A. C.
Storer, Norman W.
Twain, Mark
Untermeyer, Louis
Wilson, Woodrow
Wright, George C.

INDEX OF FIFTH LINE RHYME WORDS

Fifth Line rhymes are listed alphabetically. In parentheses are the key words under which the limericks appear. Thus, if only a Fifth Line is known ('Twas the peter of Paul the Apostle), APOSTLE (GOSSAL) indicates that the desired limerick appears under GOSSAL.